THE EVERYTHING KIDS' FAIRIES

PUZZLE and ACTIVITY BOOK

Enter the magical world of sprites, pixies, and fairy godmothers

Charles Timmerman and Calla Timmerman

Aadamsmedia

Avon, Massachusetts

EDITORIAL
Innovation Director: Paula Munier
Editorial Director: Laura M. Daly
Associate Copy Chief: Sheila Zwiebel
Acquisitions Editor: Kerry Smith
Production Editor: Casey Ebert

PRODUCTION
Director of Manufacturing: Susan Beale
Production Project Manager:
Michelle Roy Kelly
Prepress: Erick DaCosta, Matt LeBlanc
Interior Layout: Heather Barrett, Brewster Brownville,
Colleen Cunningham, Jennifer Oliveira

An Everything® Series Book.
Everything® and everything.com® are registered trademarks of F+W Publications, Inc.

Published by Adams Media, an F+W Publications Company
57 Littlefield Street, Avon, MA 02322. U.S.A.
www.adamsmedia.com

ISBN 10: 1-59869-394-8
ISBN 13: 978-1-59869-394-2

Printed in the United States of America.

J   I   H   G   F   E   D   C   B   A

This publication is designed to provide accurate and authoritative information with regard to the subject matter covered. It is sold with the understanding that the publisher is not engaged in rendering legal, accounting, or other professional advice. If legal advice or other expert assistance is required, the services of a competent professional person should be sought.

—From a *Declaration of Principles* jointly adopted by a Committee of the American Bar Association and a Committee of Publishers and Associations

Cover illustrations by Dana Regan.
Interior illustrations by Kurt Dolber and Dover.
Puzzles by Charles Timmerman.

This book is available at quantity discounts for bulk purchases.
For information, please call 1-800-289-0963.

See the entire Everything® series at www.everything.com.

Contents

Dedication

Dedicated to Calla's little sister.

Introduction

Fairy tales always have happy endings. But first there must be a challenge, something to test the main character. For example, Cinderella had to live with her mean stepmother and stepsisters before she met the prince at the ball. In Pinocchio's case, he changed into a real boy only after he learned to treat his father with respect. Good things happened to Cinderella and Pinocchio after they proved that they were worthy. In this book you will be challenged, but in a fun way. Are you ready?

Amusing math and logic puzzles will tickle your brain and try to trip you up. Clever word puzzles like crosswords, word searches, and rhyming games will do their best to stump you. Mysterious mazes and other picture puzzles will attempt to stop you in your tracks. Along the way you will meet all kinds of fairy friends. Unicorns, the tooth fairy, fairy godmothers, flower fairies, and even friendly dragons will come alive in these pages. Everyone in fairyland loves to have fun and that is the number one goal of this book. But your parents will be happy to know that your brain will be getting a healthy mental workout. And you can probably find a puzzle or two that will amuse, and maybe even stump, Mom or Dad.

So grab your magic wand (or pencil), sprinkle some fairy dust around the room, and engage your brain as we start this journey through a fairyland of puzzles. May you have fun and live happily ever after!

Find the Pictures

Can you find each of these pictures on another page of this book? There is one picture from each chapter. Write the chapter number in the space below each picture.

___

___

___

___

___

___

___

___

___

Chapter 1

Fairyland

The Path to Fairyland

Can you help this boy find the path back to his home in fairyland?

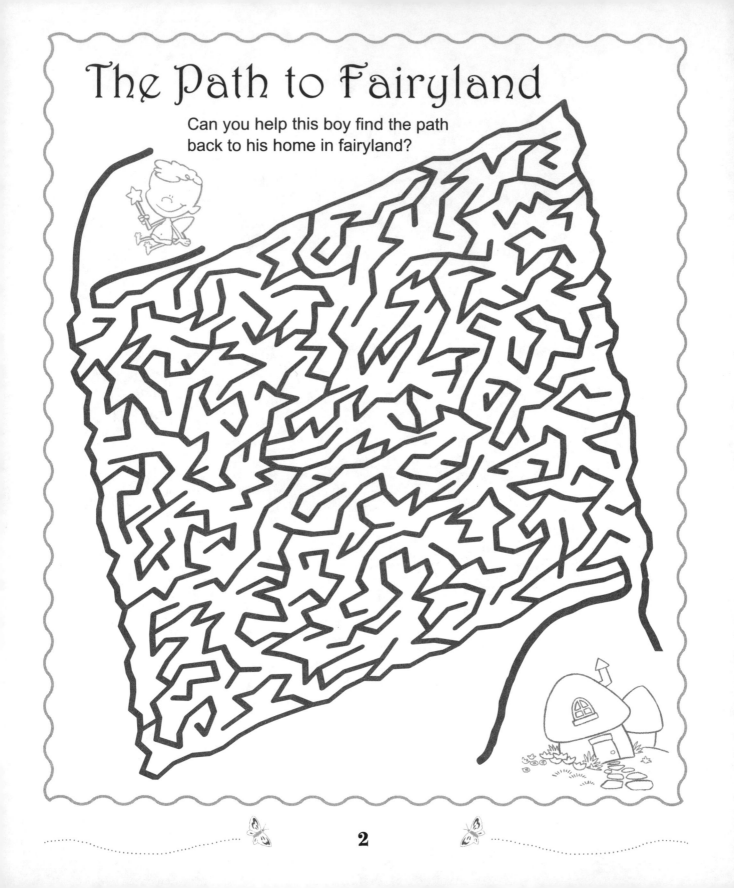

Butterfly Twins

In fairyland, every butterfly has a twin. Circle the butterflies on this page who are missing their twin.

Fairyland Photos

It's not easy to take accurate photos in fairyland! These two photos are supposed to be identical. Can you spot eight differences?

Fairy Foods

Fairies are very picky eaters. Can you find all of these fairy foods in the letters below? Look up, down, sideways, backwards, and diagonally.

BISCUIT
BREAD
CAKE
CANDY
CHEESE

CHOCOLATE
CUSTARD
GUMDROP
HONEY
LICORICE

MILK
NECTAR
NUTMEG
PECANS
PEPPERMINT

PERSIMMON
STRAWBERRY
SUGARPLUM
WHIPPED CREAM
ZUCCHINI

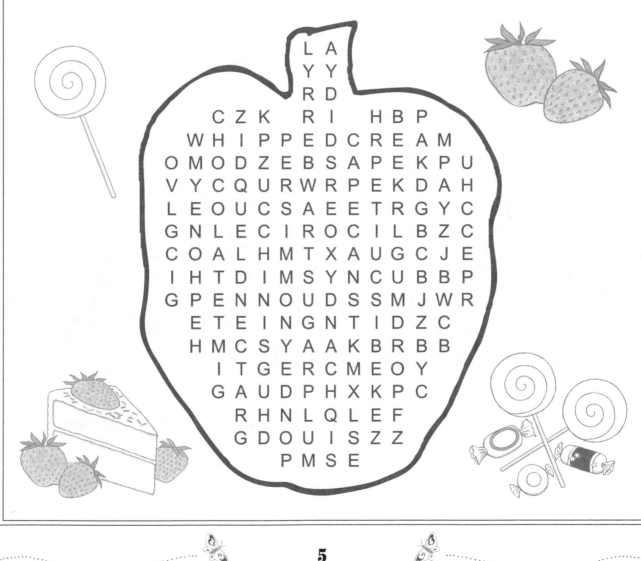

```
          L A
          Y Y D
          R D
    C Z K   R I   H B P
    W H I P P E D C R E A M
  O M O D Z E B S A P E K P U
  V Y C Q U R W R P E K D A H
  L E O U C S A E E T R G Y C
  G N L E C I R O C I L B Z C
  C O A L H M T X A U G C J E
  I H T D I M S Y N C U B B P
  G P E N N O U D S S M J W R
  E T E I N G N T I D Z C
  H M C S Y A A K B R B B
    I T G E R C M E O Y
    G A U D P H X K P C
    R H N L Q L E F
    G D O U I S Z Z
        P M S E
```

Fairy Hill

Fairies often live inside hollow hills. They need your help to complete this mathemagical home. For each empty rock below, enter the sum of the two numbers beneath it on either corner. One example is already done (5 + 4 = 9). Complete all of the rocks to the very top.

Fairyland Code

In fairyland, codes are often used to send secret messages.
Can you decode the message below using the following key?

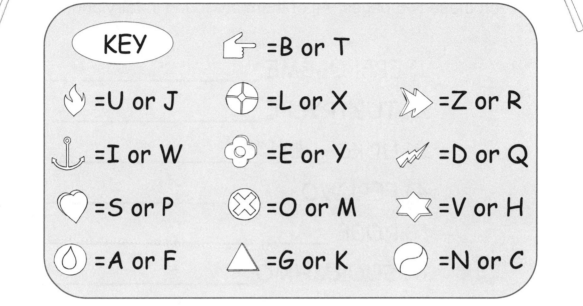

KEY

👈 =B or T

🔥 =U or J   ⊕ =L or X   ⪢ =Z or R

⚓ =I or W   ✿ =E or Y   ⚡ =D or Q

♡ =S or P   ⊗ =O or M   ✡ =V or H

💧 =A or F   △ =G or K   ◐ =N or C

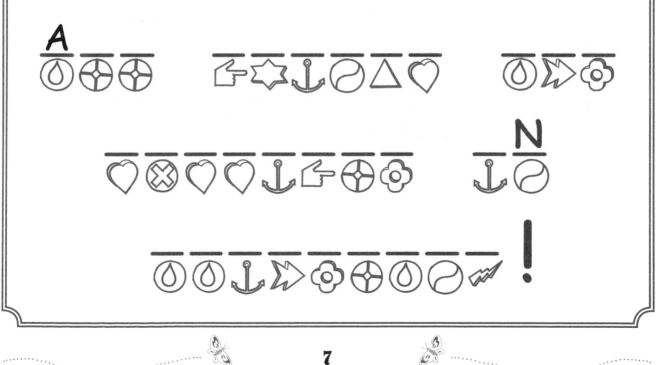

Fairyland Plants & Animals

Unscramble the letters to name the plants and animals displayed on these two pages. All of them are found in fairyland!

1) EBELUBBME _____

2) TUBTRYLFE _____

3) UDKC __DUCK_____

4) FERLWO _____

5) ROGF _____

6) SUORMHMO _____

7) NASIL _____

8) IBDR _____

9) ONOCRAC _____

10) EERT _____

Fit all of the unscrambled plant and animal names into this clueless crossword puzzle. Each word is used only once, and must fit exactly into the number of boxes.

D U C K

The Language of Fairyland

Fairies love to make rhymes! Use the given
clues to determine pairs of words that rhyme.

A playground for a
toothy ocean animal is a:

_ _ _ _ _   _ _ _ _ _

For example:

A gorilla garment is an:

<u>APE</u> <u>CAPE</u>

A rodent abode is a:

_ _ _ _ _   _ _ _ _

A birthday treat for
a scaly friend is a:

_ _ _ _ _   _ _ _ _

A utensil to eat a
dried plum is a:

_ _ _ _ _   _ _ _ _ _

Triangle Mushrooms

Fairyland is filled with mushrooms. Can you help this fairy find these mushrooms on this page?

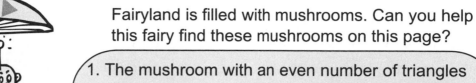

1. The mushroom with an even number of triangles
2. The mushroom with the least number of triangles
3. The mushroom with exactly seven triangles
4. The mushroom with the most number of triangles

Fairyland Riddles

I'm found in the fairy forest
and I end with an E;
I provide plenty of shade,
and you can climb on me.
Draw a picture of what I am:

I'm red and I'm tasty
and I start with an A;
fairyland teachers love me,
and I keep the doctor away.
Draw a picture of what I am:

Flowers & Mushrooms

Draw two flowers and three mushrooms in the boxes below.
No flower should be next to another flower.
No mushroom should be next to another mushroom.

Chapter 2

Fairy Godmothers

Directions Home

In many stories, fairy godmothers give advice and direction. Can you pick the one set of directions that will lead the beetle home through this flower maze?

U=move up   D=move down   L=move left   R=move right

A) U, R, R, D, R, U, U, U, U, L, L, U   C) U, R, R, D, R, R, U, U, U, L, U, U

B) U, R, R, D, R, R, U, U, U, D, L, U   D) U, R, R, D, R, R, U, U, U, L, L, U

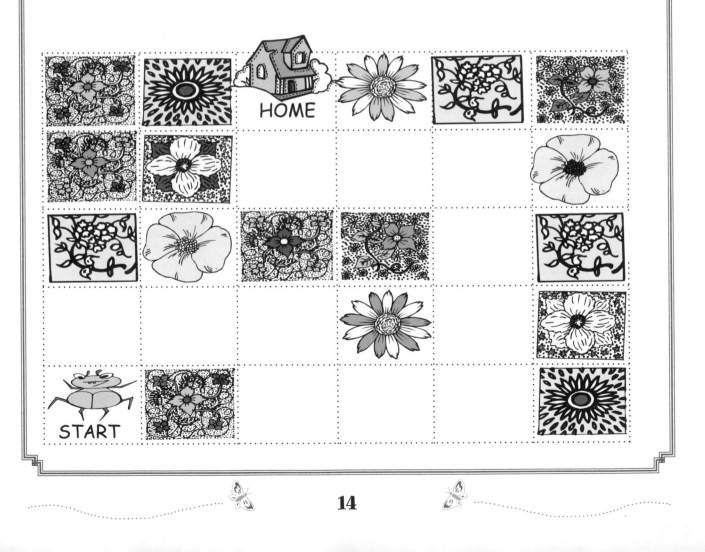

Fairy Dust Letters

Help fairy godmother sprinkle these letters to form animal names. Each group of letters will be used only once to complete the name of an animal.

MST IG RB CU LP NOC RA BR RS YO PA PM ETA ABB CCO GEH EPH GU M POP

POR_____PINE   GE_____IL
LEO_____RD   CHE_____H
HO_____E   CHI_____UNK
RHI_____EROS   JA_____AR
RA_____ON   HED_____OG
ZE_____A   HA_____ER
R_____IT   HIP_____OTAMUS
EL_____ANT   T_____ER
GI_____FFE   DO_____HIN
CA_____EL   CO_____TE

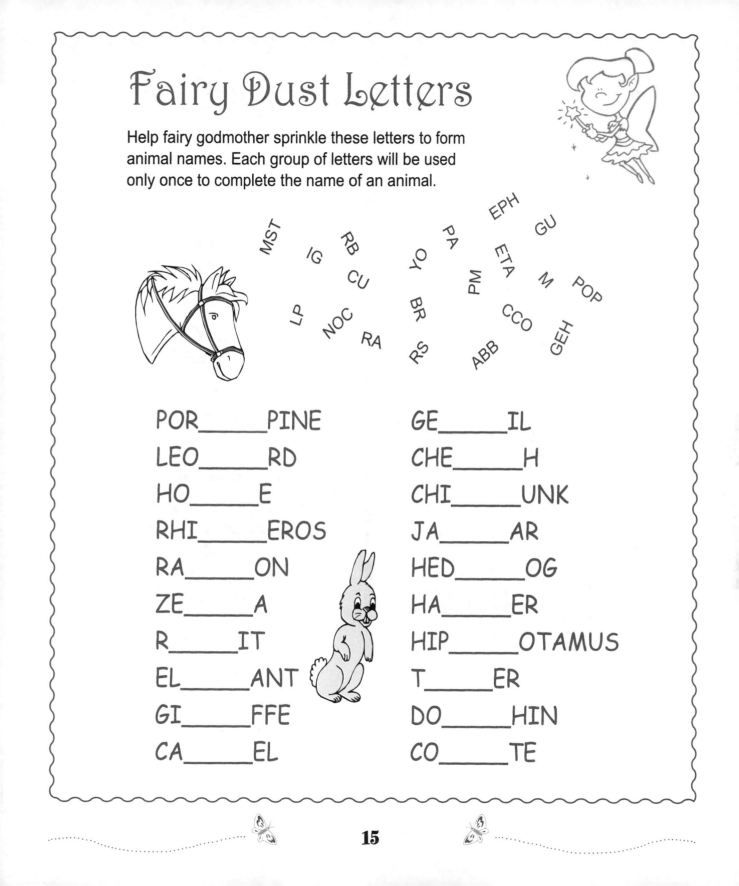

Magical Changes

Fairy godmothers know how to magically change things.
Change these words into other words by rearranging the letters.

For example:
Rearrange the letters in the
word **gum** and make this:

M U G

Rearrange the letters in the
word **art** and make this:

— — —

Rearrange the letters in the
word **disk** and make these:

— — — —

Rearrange the letters in the
word **flea** and make this:

— — — —

Rearrange the letters in the word **fowl** and make this:

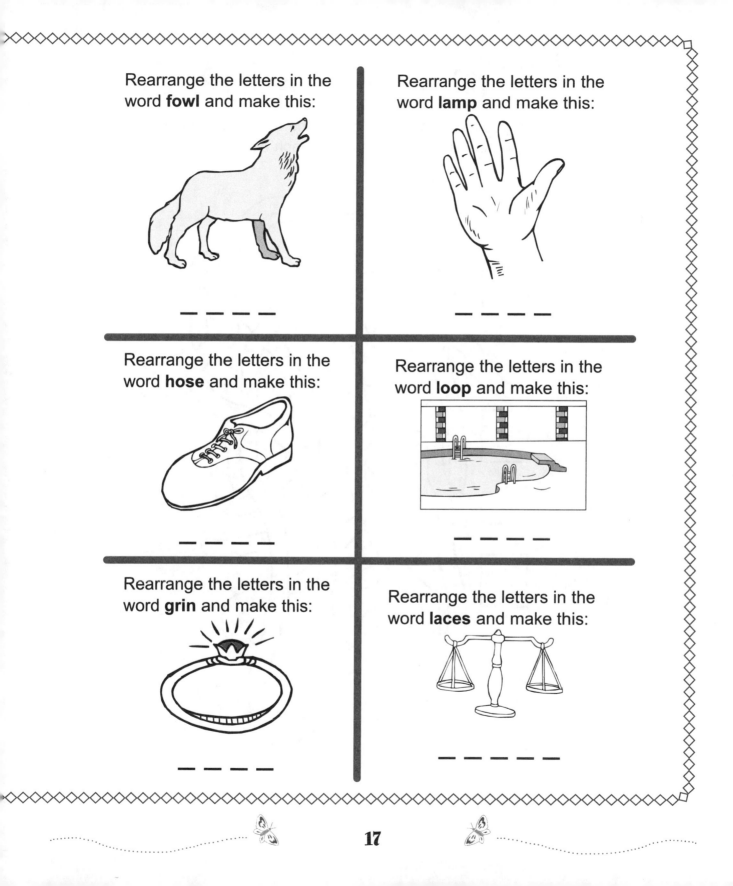

_ _ _ _

Rearrange the letters in the word **lamp** and make this:

_ _ _ _

Rearrange the letters in the word **hose** and make this:

_ _ _ _

Rearrange the letters in the word **loop** and make this:

_ _ _ _

Rearrange the letters in the word **grin** and make this:

_ _ _ _

Rearrange the letters in the word **laces** and make this:

_ _ _ _ _

Whose Wand?

Can you help these fairy godmothers get their wands?
Put the correct wand number in each box.

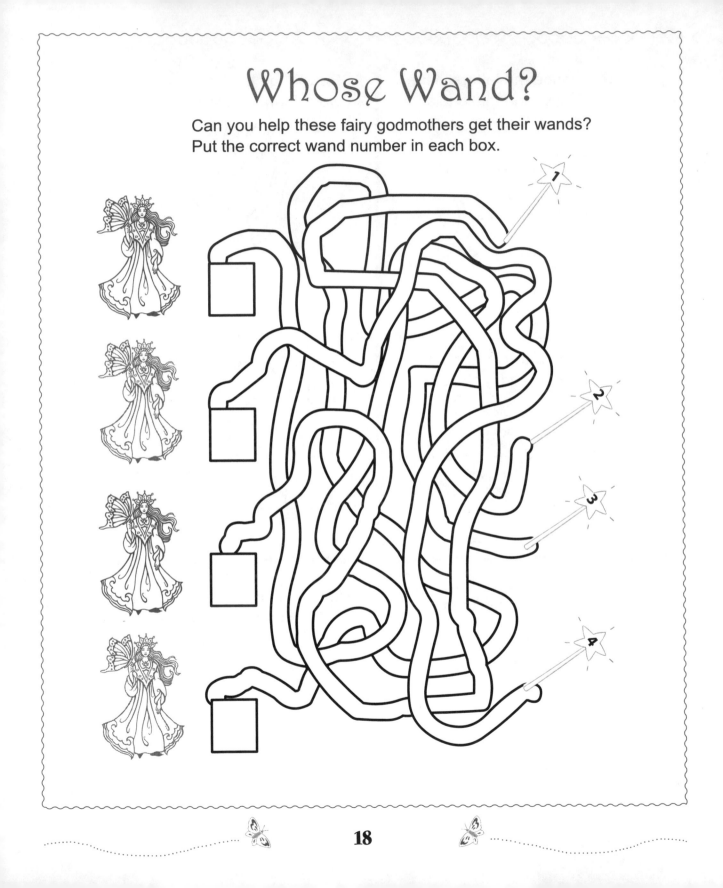

Break the Spell

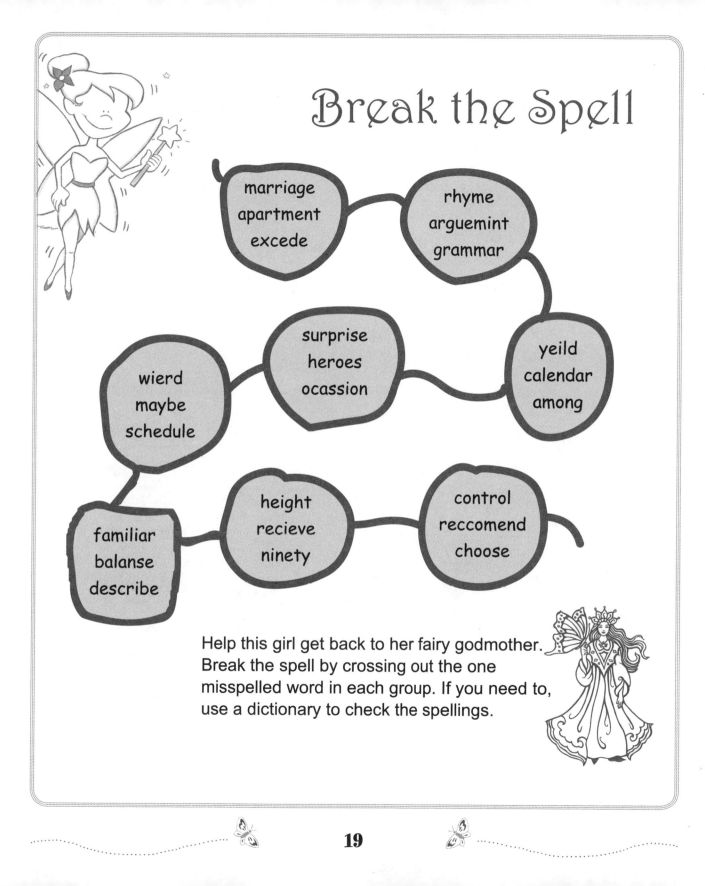

marriage
apartment
excede

rhyme
arguemint
grammar

surprise
heroes
ocassion

yeild
calendar
among

wierd
maybe
schedule

height
recieve
ninety

control
reccomend
choose

familiar
balanse
describe

Help this girl get back to her fairy godmother.
Break the spell by crossing out the one
misspelled word in each group. If you need to,
use a dictionary to check the spellings.

Cinderella's Glass Slipper

The fairy godmother has made a glass slipper for Cinderella. Follow the clues to help Cinderella figure out which shoe is her glass slipper.

Cinderella's glass slipper is in a column that also has a bird.

Cinderella's glass slipper is not in the first column.

Cinderella's glass slipper is in a row that also has a pumpkin.

Cinderella's Magic Time

The fairy godmother's magic spell ends at midnight! Rank each clock by the amount of time it shows remaining until midnight. Start by putting a 1 next to the clock with the most time remaining.

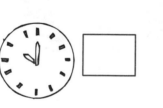

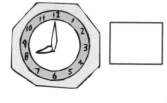

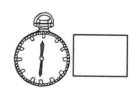

Riddles

Just for fun, your fairy godmother has prepared these riddles for you! Translate the answers using this code: 1 = A, 2 = B, 3 = C, etc.

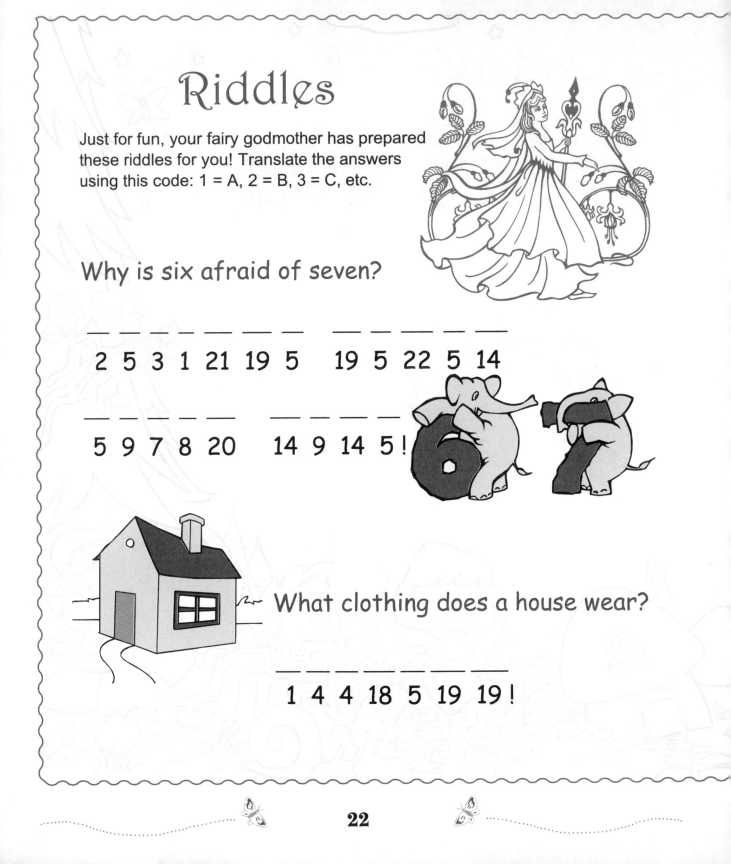

Why is six afraid of seven?

___ ___ ___ ___ ___ ___ ___   ___ ___ ___ ___ ___
2   5   3   1   21 19 5   19 5   22 5   14

___ ___ ___ ___ ___   ___ ___ ___ ___ !
5   9   7   8   20   14 9   14 5

What clothing does a house wear?

___ ___ ___ ___ ___ ___ ___ !
1   4   4   18 5   19 19

What is in the middle of Paris?

$\overline{20}\ \overline{8}\ \overline{5}$ $\overline{12}\ \overline{5}\ \overline{20}\ \overline{20}\ \overline{5}\ \overline{18}$ $\overline{18}$!

What happens when an egg laughs?

$\overline{9}\ \overline{20}$ $\overline{3}\ \overline{18}\ \overline{1}\ \overline{3}\ \overline{11}\ \overline{19}$ $\overline{21}\ \overline{16}$!

What month has 28 days?

$\overline{1}\ \overline{12}\ \overline{12}$ $\overline{15}\ \overline{6}$ $\overline{20}\ \overline{8}\ \overline{5}\ \overline{13}$!

What has four legs but only one foot?

$\overline{1}$ $\overline{2}\ \overline{5}\ \overline{4}$!

What's Next?

Fairy godmothers can often predict the future. Can you predict the next number in these sequences? Hint: look for a pattern.

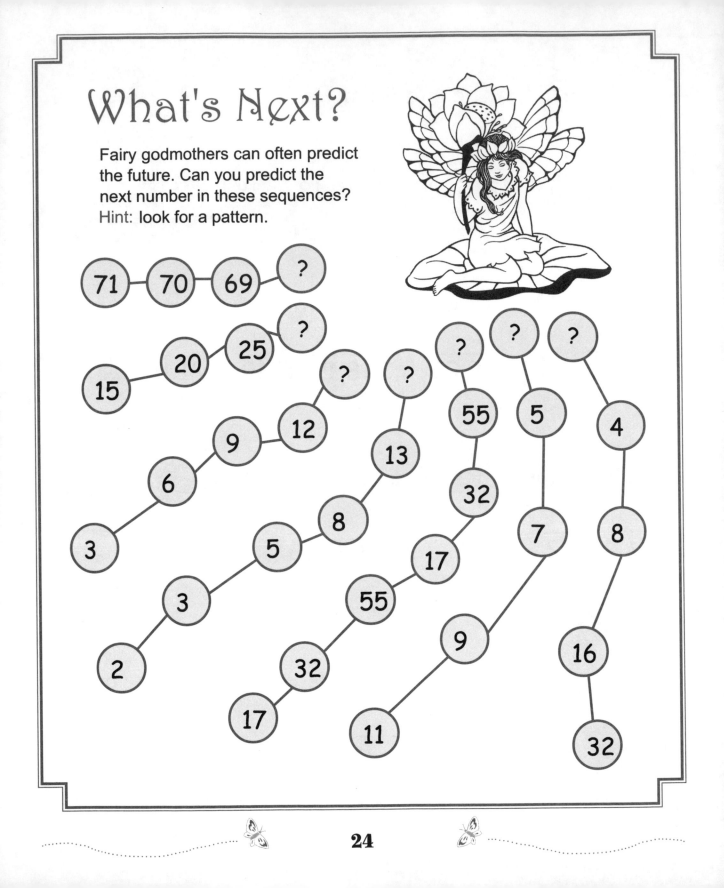

71 — 70 — 69 — ?

15 — 20 — 25 — ?

3 — 6 — 9 — 12 — ?

2 — 3 — 5 — 8 — 13 — ?

17 — 32 — 55 — 8 — 5 — 17 — 32 — 55 — ?

11 — 9 — 7 — 5 — ?

32 — 16 — 8 — 4 — ?

Chapter 3
Flower Fairies

Flower Maze

Can you help the flower fairy
find a path through this flower?

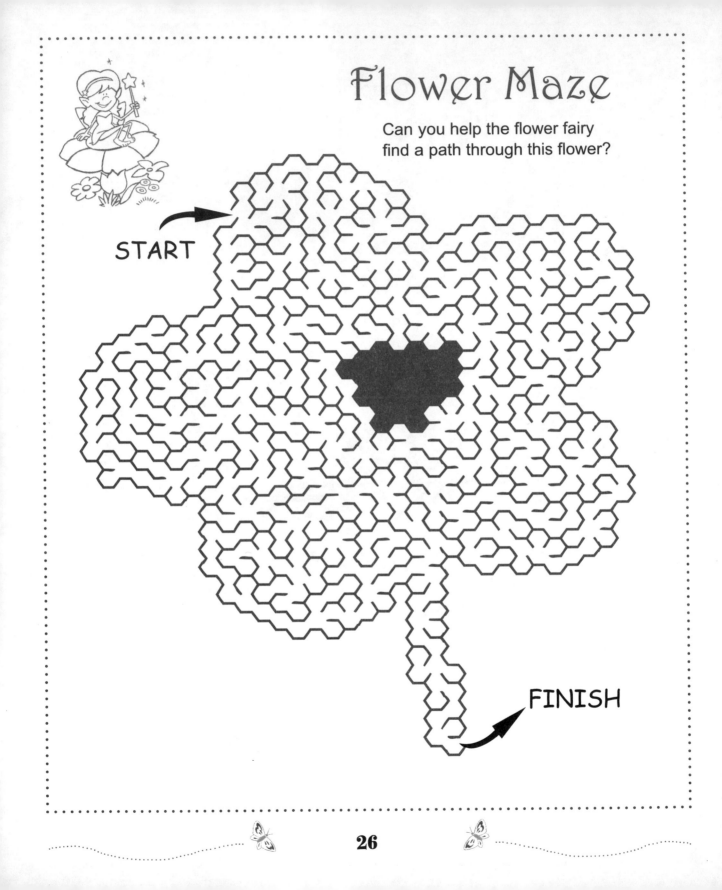

START

FINISH

A Flower Fairy Christmas

The flower fairy has a Christmas present for you! To find out what it is, cross out all of these letters from the grid: U V W X Y Z

WZPXYWYOUU
IVUZZNXYSZ
EWTZTXWIXA

Flowery Dividers

Draw three straight lines that will separate each flower into its own section. Hint: think triangle.

Flower Values

Help the fairies determine the values of these sets of flowers. Rank them from 1 to 4, from most to least valuable.

Here is a guide to help you determine the relative values:

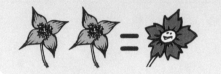 

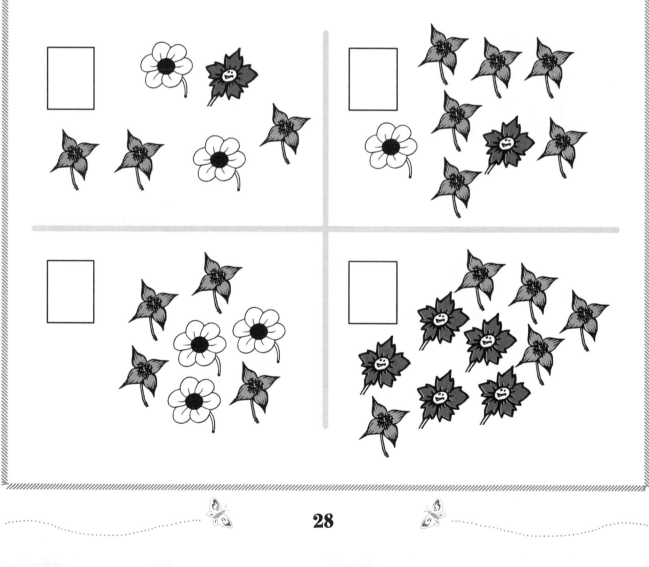

The Flower Fairy Garden

Change one letter in each capitalized word so that the sentences will make sense.

1. LATER makes the garden grow. _____

2. Besides flowers, the fairies also grow HORN. _____

3. The fairies use a HOG to help plant their garden. _____

4. The HUGS were asked to please not eat the flowers! _____

5. In the spring, the fairies plant SLEDS in the garden. _____

6. The TOPSAIL is just right to grow flowers. _____

7. Use your NOTE to smell the fragrant flowers. _____

Smart Shopper

Help the flower fairy figure out which price is the best buy for each flower.

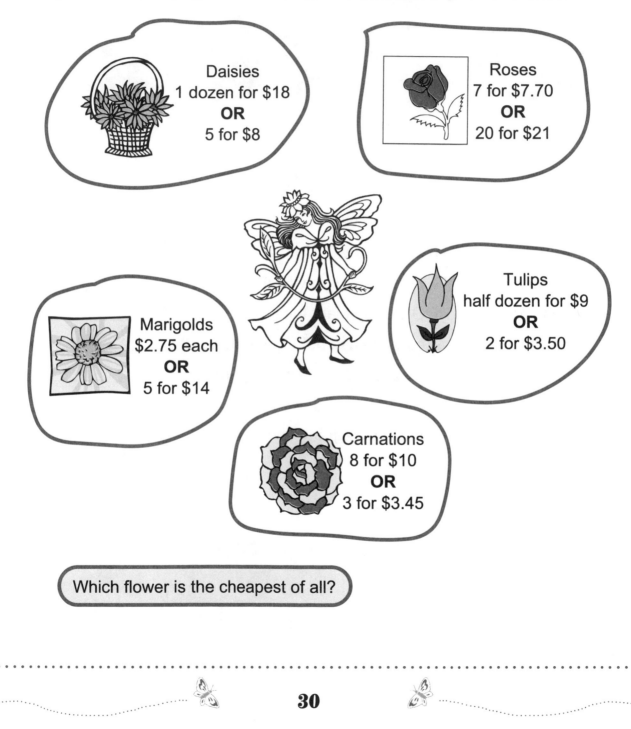

Daisies
1 dozen for $18
OR
5 for $8

Roses
7 for $7.70
OR
20 for $21

Marigolds
$2.75 each
OR
5 for $14

Tulips
half dozen for $9
OR
2 for $3.50

Carnations
8 for $10
OR
3 for $3.45

Which flower is the cheapest of all?

OWER Words

The word *flower* ends with the letters OWER. Fill in the blanks to make more words that end with OWER.

_ _ _ _ _ _ _ O W E R

_ _ O W E R

_ _ O W E R

_ _ _ O W E R

_ _ _ _ _ _ O W E R

Flower Riddles

Answer the clues below and fill the letters into the grid. Work back and forth between the grid and the clues until you figure it out.

Why couldn't the flower ride its bike?

1D	2C	3C	4D	5E	6E	7D		8E	9B
10D	11C	12C	13D		14B	15E	16B		
17A	18A	19C	20A	21C	22E	!			

C. A place for coats.

___ ___ ___ ___ ___ ___
3   21 11 12 2 19

A. Vegetable found in a pod.

___ ___ ___
17 18 20

B. What do you do on a chair?

___ ___ ___
16 14 9

D. Something with four legs.

___ ___ ___ ___ ___
13 4 1 10 7

E. Clubs, diamonds, hearts, and spades.

___ ___ ___ ___ ___
6 5 8 15 22

_____

> If April showers bring May flowers, what do May flowers bring?

Flower Equations

Can you help the flower fairy figure out what numbers should go in the boxes to complete these equations?

=5

=20

=25

-8

+19

+□

+□

+12

+61

7

□

-73

Flowery Search

Can you find all of the flowers in the letters below?
Look up, down, sideways, backwards, and diagonally.

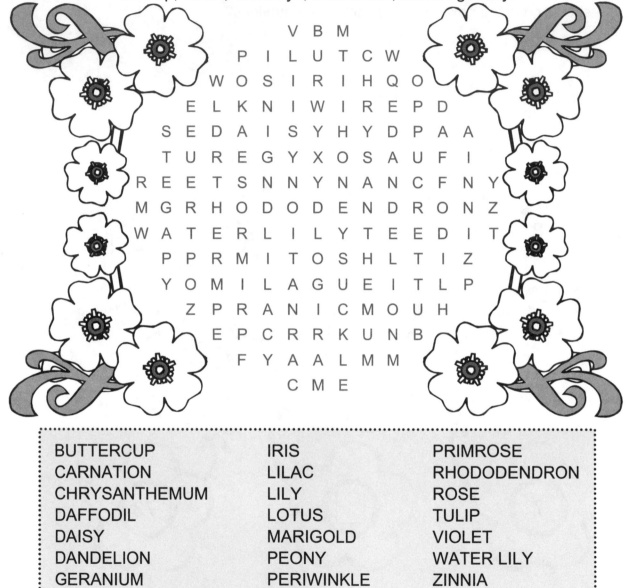

```
            V  B  M
         P  I  L  U  T  C  W
      W  O  S  I  R  I  H  Q  O
      E  L  K  N  I  W  I  R  E  P  D
      S  E  D  A  I  S  Y  H  Y  D  P  A  A
      T  U  R  E  G  Y  X  O  S  A  U  F  I
      R  E  E  T  S  N  N  Y  N  A  N  C  F  N  Y
      M  G  R  H  O  D  O  D  E  N  D  R  O  N  Z
      W  A  T  E  R  L  I  L  Y  T  E  E  D  I  T
      P  P  R  M  I  T  O  S  H  L  T  I  Z
      Y  O  M  I  L  A  G  U  E  I  T  L  P
      Z  P  R  A  N  I  C  M  O  U  H
      E  P  C  R  R  K  U  N  B
      F  Y  A  A  L  M  M
            C  M  E
```

BUTTERCUP	IRIS	PRIMROSE
CARNATION	LILAC	RHODODENDRON
CHRYSANTHEMUM	LILY	ROSE
DAFFODIL	LOTUS	TULIP
DAISY	MARIGOLD	VIOLET
DANDELION	PEONY	WATER LILY
GERANIUM	PERIWINKLE	ZINNIA
HONEYSUCKLE	POPPY	

Flower Fairy Delivery

The flower fairy brings you one of these flowers every day except Wednesday:

The flower fairy brings you one of these flowers on days that start with the letter T (like Tuesday):

The flower fairy brings you one of these flowers on days that have six letters (like Monday):

What flowers will you have from the Monday through Friday deliveries?

A.   B.   C.

Fractured Flowers

Help the fairy put these flowers together again by drawing a line connecting the two halves of each flower.

Fairy Tales

Antique Books

Most fairy tales are very old and have been told for generations. These antique books are well-worn. Fill in the missing letters and reveal the fairy tale titles.

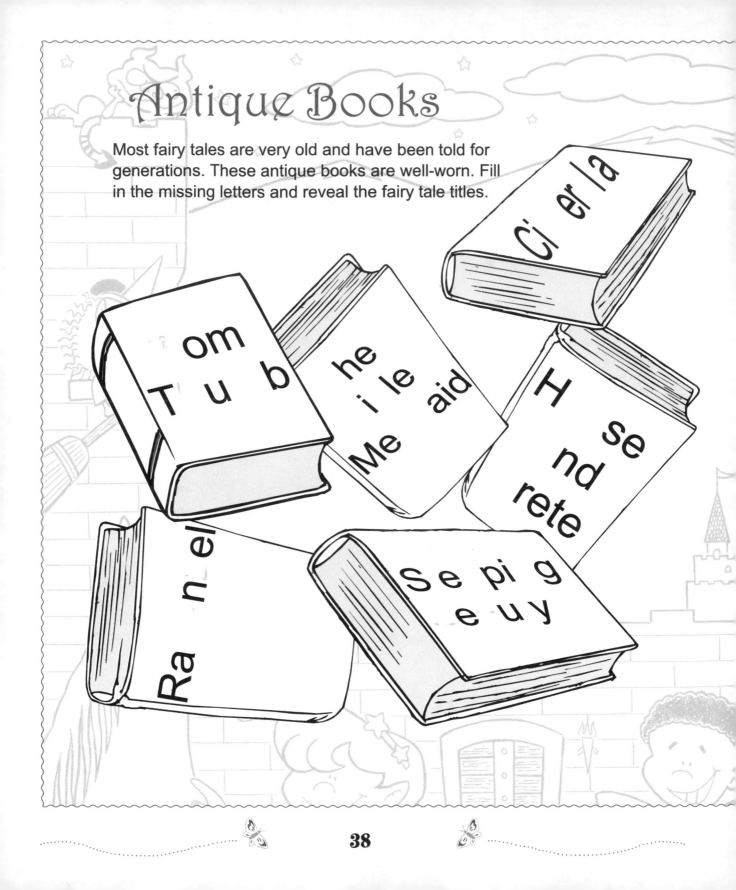

Ci er la

om
T u b

he
i le
Me aid

H se
nd
rete

Ra n el

Se pi g
e u y

Three Bears' Bingo

In this version of the fairy tale, Goldilocks finds bingo cards for the three bears. Solve the equations and cross out the answers on the cards. The winner is the card with four answers in a row across, down, or diagonally. Which bear wins?

17 + 3 = _____

11 + 11 = _____

11 + 17 + 8 = _____

9 + 8 + 7 = _____

33 + 28 + 33 = _____

82 - 4 = _____

93 - 9 = _____

78 - 11 = _____

56 ÷ 8 = _____

10 X 5 = _____

5 X 9 = _____

34 ÷ 2 = _____

26 ÷ 13 = _____

4 X 11 = _____

90 ÷ 9 = _____

27 - 8 = _____

10 + 20 + 7 = _____

25 ÷ 5 = _____

37 - 26 = _____

2 X 7 = _____

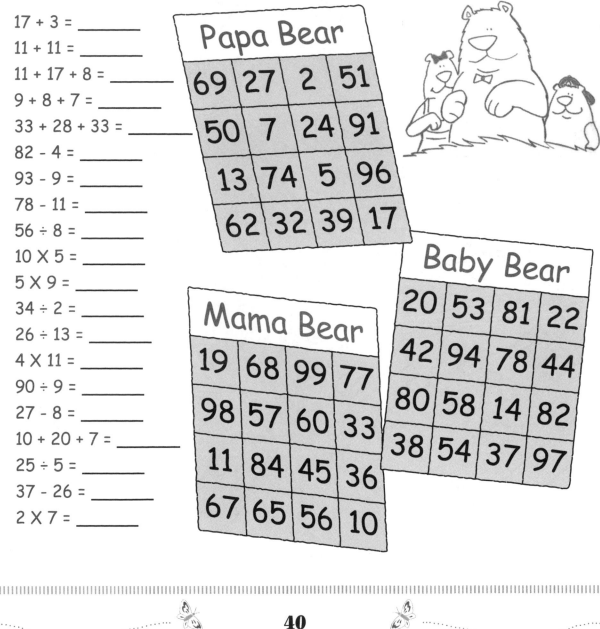

Papa Bear

69	27	2	51
50	7	24	91
13	74	5	96
62	32	39	17

Mama Bear

19	68	99	77
98	57	60	33
11	84	45	36
67	65	56	10

Baby Bear

20	53	81	22
42	94	78	44
80	58	14	82
38	54	37	97

Rapunzel's Hair Connection

The Prince needs to know which strand of hair belongs to Rapunzel.
In each box, write the name of the person connected to it by their hair.

Ursula   Rapunzel   Trixy   Glenda

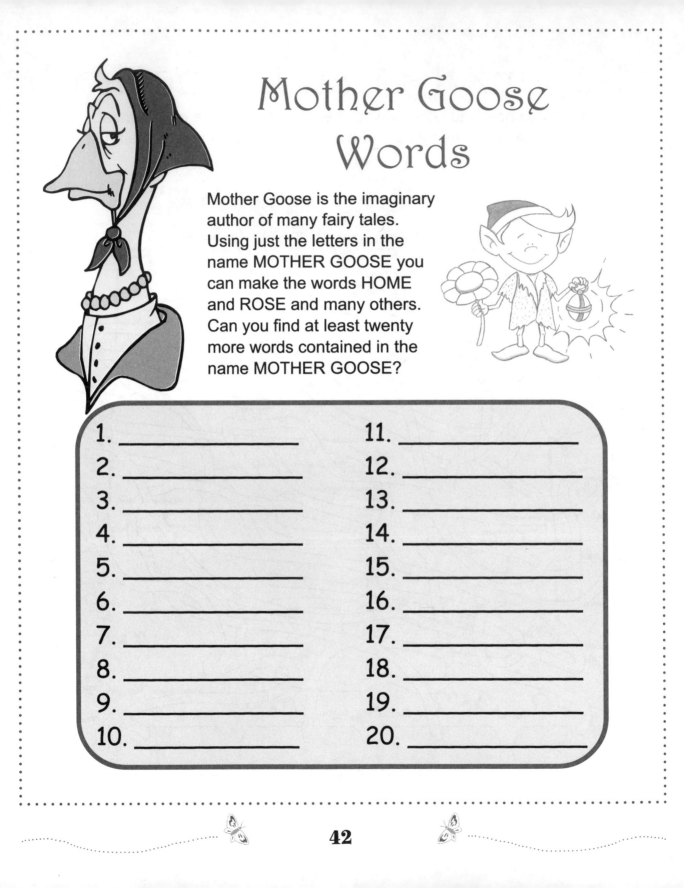

Mother Goose Words

Mother Goose is the imaginary author of many fairy tales. Using just the letters in the name MOTHER GOOSE you can make the words HOME and ROSE and many others. Can you find at least twenty more words contained in the name MOTHER GOOSE?

1. _____
2. _____
3. _____
4. _____
5. _____
6. _____
7. _____
8. _____
9. _____
10. _____

11. _____
12. _____
13. _____
14. _____
15. _____
16. _____
17. _____
18. _____
19. _____
20. _____

The Prince's Real Clothes

The emperor needs your help to find his real clothes.
Circle the suit with these characteristics:

1. Buttons on the jacket.
2. No stripes on the tie.
2. Stars on the jacket.
3. No flower.

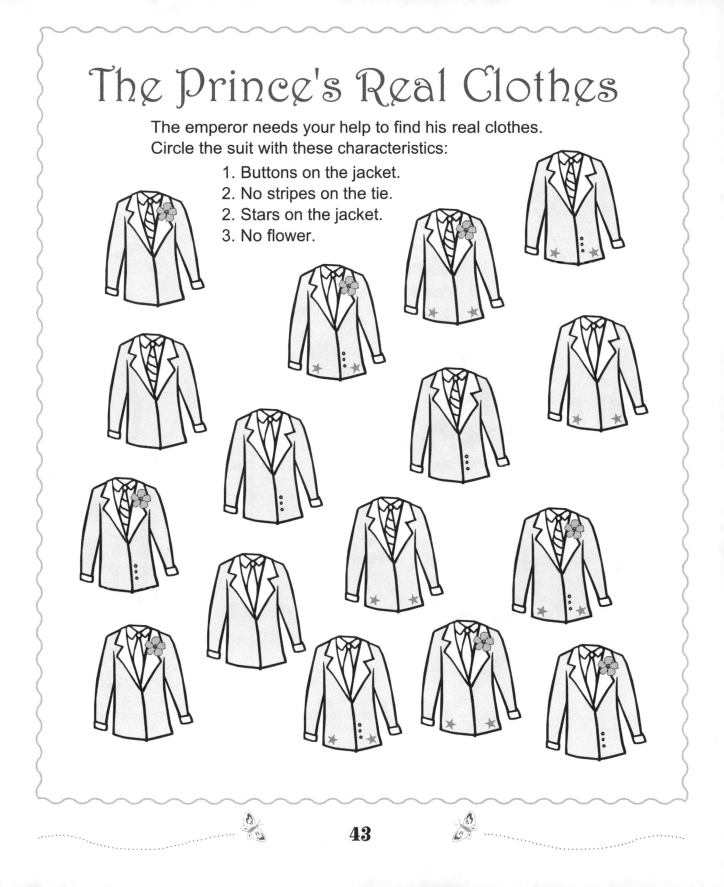

Hansel & Gretel

Can you help Hansel and Gretel find the gingerbread house? They dropped three of each of these charms on the only safe path:

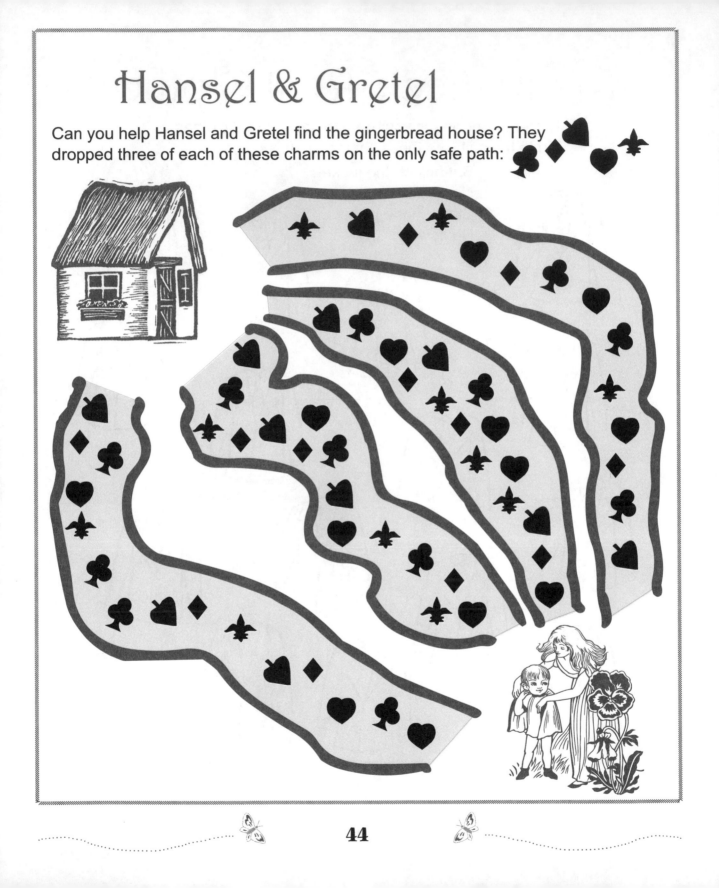

The Gingerbread House

Hansel and Gretel are looking for candy! Find three groups of candy on the roof that look like these:

The Three Little Pigs

Reassemble these pieces of a sign to find out the address of the little piggy who built his house out of straw.

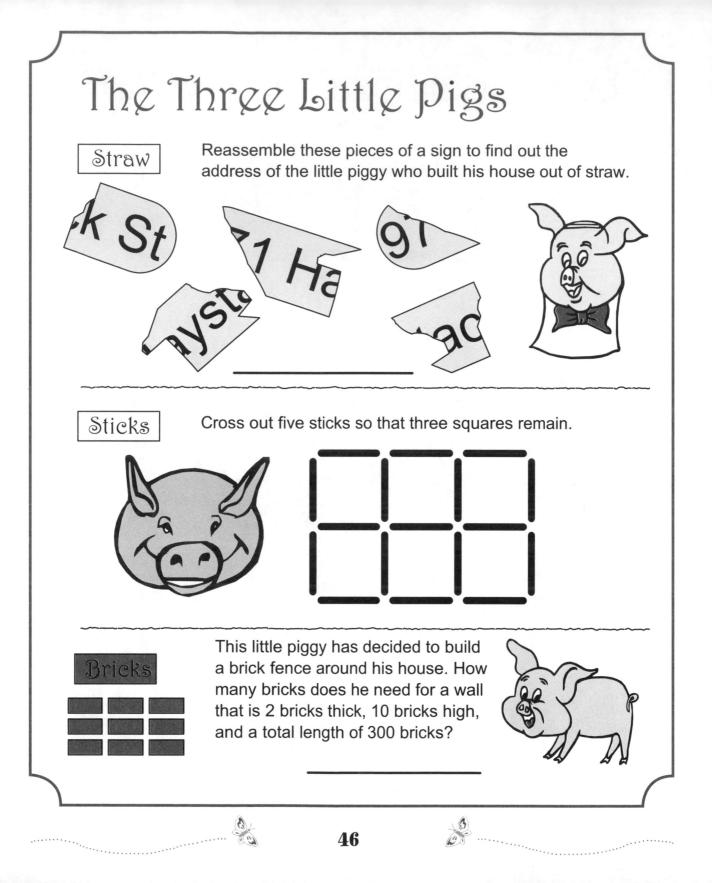

k St

91

71 Ha

ays

ac

_____

Sticks

Cross out five sticks so that three squares remain.

Bricks

This little piggy has decided to build a brick fence around his house. How many bricks does he need for a wall that is 2 bricks thick, 10 bricks high, and a total length of 300 bricks?

_____

The Princess and the Pea

The Princess and the Pea is a Danish fairy tale by Hans Christian Andersen. All of the answers to this puzzle should contain these letters together: **PEA**. Fill in the blanks to name each picture.

For example:

SPEAKER

_ _ _ _ _

_ _ _ _ _

_ _ _ _ _ _ _

_ _ _ _

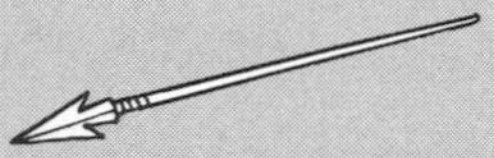

_ _ _ _

_ _ _ _ _

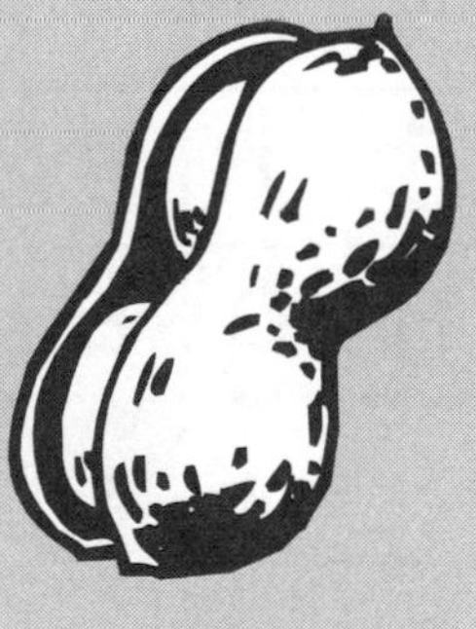

_ _ _ _ _ _

Wedding Bells

Often a fairy tale will end with a wedding. Circle the three fragments below that can be put together to make these wedding bells:

The End...

Figure out where to put each of the scrambled letters. They all fit in the spaces directly underneath. When you have filled in the grid correctly, you will see the line that ends many fairy tales.

	N	A		R									
A	F	T	P	R	H	L	Y		E	V	Y	R	
A	H	D	E	T	I	E	Y		L	I	E	E	D
											V		
				P									
A													

Chapter 5
Unicorns

Latin Unicorn

In Latin, *UNI* means one and *CORN* means horn.
Put them together and you get a word that means one horn.

Figure out these words that also start with *UNI*:

one wheel:
U N I _ _ _ _ _ _

one outfit:
U N I _ _ _ _

together as one:
U N I _ _ _

one sound:
U N I _ _ _

Unscramble these letters, add them to CORN, and make a type of horn. If you need to, use a dictionary to help figure this one out:

C O R N _ _ _ _ _ _ _

A I U
P O C

Secret Message

Decode this message to find out what the unicorn said to Alice in the story *Through the Looking-Glass* by Lewis Carroll. Every letter is coded as the next letter in the alphabet. For example, HELLO is coded as IFMMP.

JG ZPV'MM CFMJFWF JO NF, J'MM CFMJFWF JO ZPV.

Unicorn Healers

Unicorns are known for their mystical healing abilities. Separate the "sick" words from the "well" words by drawing one horizontal line and one vertical line.

hardy   bright-eyed   vigorous   chipper   queasy   frail   feeble

flourishing

wholesome   bushy-tailed   bedridden   nauseated

strong   weak

lousy   ill   feverish   ailing   impaired   hospitalized   rotten   robust   fit

Horse Barn

Unicorns are pretend creatures with the body of a horse and a head with a horn. Can you find all of these real horse breeds in the letters below? Look up, down, sideways, backward, and diagonally.

Appaloosa
Arabian
Ardennes
Azteca
Bashkir
Clydesdale
Fleuve
Holsteiner
Konik
Lokai
Morgan
Mustang
Noriker
Palomino
Percheron
Salerno
Sardinian
Thoroughbred
Tinker
Walkaloosa

```
S A R D I N I A N I U T D X G
R R E R E K I R O N H E U U I
B E S E N N E D R A R L S N F
C K O N I K B S E B C A X G Q
P N A I B A R A H A A D W B Q
A I I S S D M G C L C S R B M
A T A H O L U W R A W E M B O
D S K S R O V O E Y N D T O R
T I O A R Z L V P I L Y D Z G
R I L O L Q U A E E C L B S A
Y W H F L E R T K H C C B I N
I T E E L A S S A L E R N O W
M W U F K L P A G N A T S U M
S N P Q O X Q P W L C W A T K
F G P H L V O P A L O M I N O
```

Hidden Horns

In each sentence, read between the words to find an animal that has horns. For example, this sentence has a yak hidden in it: *Surprisingly, Akron was a great place for the alligator to live.*

Rather than have a big wedding, the elephant eloped with his bride.

The melodic owl played trumpet in the band.

The monkey ate a mango atop the house.

Suzy has been a film buff a long time and loves romantic comedies.

Be a Deer

Fill in the blanks: A deer's horns are called _____. They are made of _____ and are shed and regrown each _____.

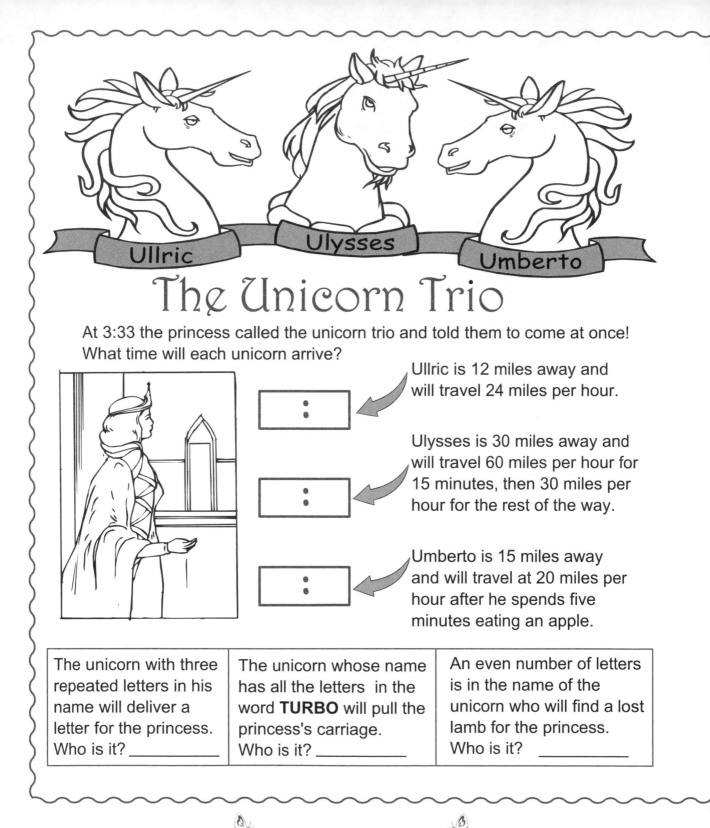

The Unicorn Trio

Ullric   Ulysses   Umberto

At 3:33 the princess called the unicorn trio and told them to come at once!
What time will each unicorn arrive?

Ullric is 12 miles away and will travel 24 miles per hour.

Ulysses is 30 miles away and will travel 60 miles per hour for 15 minutes, then 30 miles per hour for the rest of the way.

Umberto is 15 miles away and will travel at 20 miles per hour after he spends five minutes eating an apple.

The unicorn with three repeated letters in his name will deliver a letter for the princess. Who is it? _____	The unicorn whose name has all the letters in the word **TURBO** will pull the princess's carriage. Who is it? _____	An even number of letters is in the name of the unicorn who will find a lost lamb for the princess. Who is it? _____

Lunch Time!

Ullric has an apple in his lunch box.
Ulysses has three different items in his lunch box.
Umberto does not have corn in his lunch box.
Label each lunch box with the name of the unicorn:

  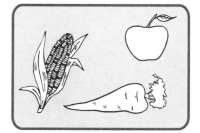

_____   _____   _____

Better Barns

Umberto's barn has a star on it.
Ulysses' barn has a heart on it.
Ullric's barn is not next to Umberto's barn.
Label each barn with the name of the unicorn:

_____   _____   _____

Shadow of a Unicorn

Circle the shadow that exactly matches this unicorn.

Unicorn Twin

Circle the unicorn that is the exact twin of the unicorn at the top of this page.

Maiden's Song

Help the unicorn find the path to the maiden.

Portrait of a Unicorn

Copy each of the nine squares from the next page into this grid.
The letters and numbers tell you where each square belongs.
Complete the portrait by coloring the picture.

	A	B	C
1			
2			
3			

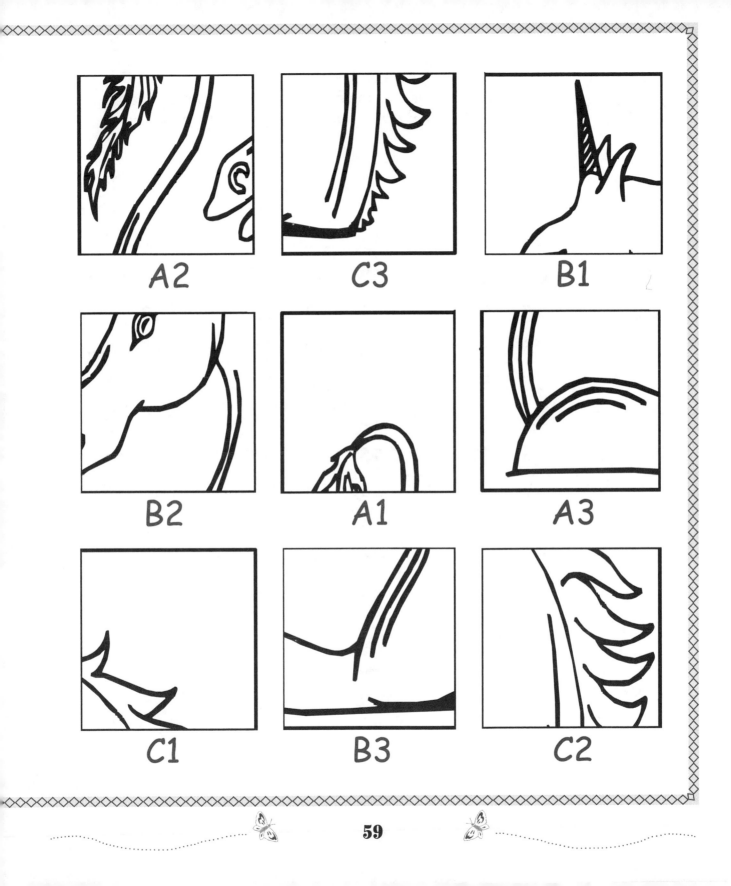

A2

C3

B1

B2

A1

A3

C1

B3

C2

Going Up

Find a path for the unicorn from 1 to 99. Each step must be to a greater number and can be up, down, left, or right, but not diagonally.

FINISH

2	31	64	79	75	94	37	69	19	72	99
22	6	66	56	45	55	67	43	45	54	96
86	34	76	62	66	67	73	75	77	87	90
80	31	75	60	19	81	59	96	94	86	84
48	35	65	55	53	50	36	18	10	92	50
22	33	31	61	60	49	71	14	84	30	69
11	91	66	42	85	45	44	43	41	39	81
10	97	51	33	85	10	40	55	70	38	87
9	15	19	22	25	54	54	16	25	36	72
7	20	25	33	28	29	30	31	33	35	71
1	21	19	45	47	55	56	57	59	63	65

START

60

Chapter 6

The Tooth Fairy

Tooth Fairy Animal

Solve this puzzle to find out what animal takes the place of the tooth fairy in some countries.

1. The first letter is in *mother* but not *brother*.
2. The second letter is in *bowl* and *spoon*.
3. The third letter comes before **V W X**.
4. The fourth letter is in the middle of *himself*.
5. The fifth letter is the fifth in the alphabet.

___	___	___	___	___
1	2	3	4	5

Baby Teeth

Solve this crazy formula to determine the total number of baby teeth for each person.

number of colors in the U.S. flag
- number of cups in a pint
+ number of seconds in a minute
- even number between 2 and 5
- number of cents in a quarter
- number of inches in a foot
_____
= total number of baby teeth

A Healthy Smile

Can you find all of these dental words in the letters below?
Look up, down, sideways, backwards, and diagonally.

floss	dentist	smile	enamel	chew	lip
toothpaste	molar	jaw	incisor	cuspid	gums
brush	decay	bite	cavity	checkup	mouth

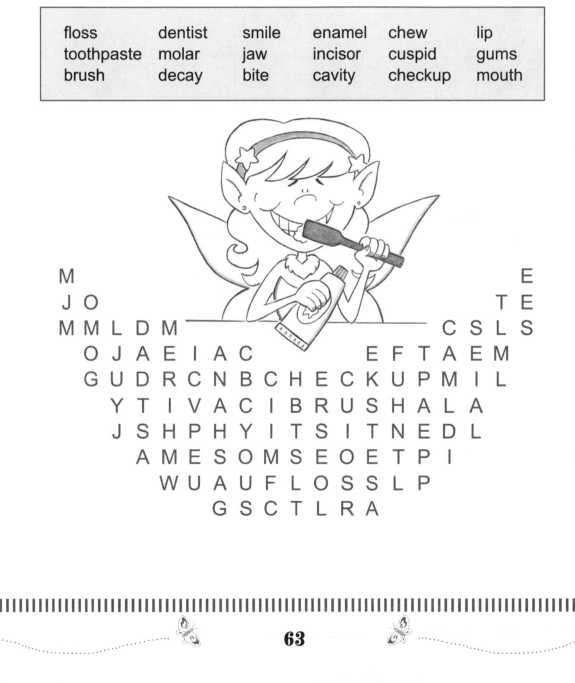

```
M                                               E
  J O                                         T   E
M M L D M                           C S L   S
  O J A E I A C               E F T A E M
  G U D R C N B C H E C K U P M I L
  Y T I V A C I B R U S H A L A
  J S H P H Y I T S I T N E D L
    A M E S O M S E O E T P I
      W U A U F L O S S L P
        G S C T L R A
```

Sweet Tooth

Complete this crossword puzzle using the pictures as clues.

The tooth fairy says, "Brush your teeth to prevent tooth decay, especially after eating sweet treats!"

A Good Deal

The tooth fairy has offered George a choice of two deals for his eight remaining baby teeth:

> 25 cents for each tooth

OR

> 1 cent for the first tooth
> 2 cents for the second tooth
> 4 cents for the third tooth
> and so on, with the payment
> doubling for each new tooth

Which deal will give George the most money for his eight teeth? _____
How much money will George receive? _____

Fast Fairy

It takes the tooth fairy 7 minutes for each tooth collected. The tooth fairy starts at 11:24 p.m. and has 19 teeth to collect. At what time will the tooth fairy be done?

_____

🦷 Step by Step 🦷

Follow these steps to convert *tooth* into *coin*.

Step 1. Drop a letter from TOOTH and get the sound of a horn:

__ __ __ __

Step 2. Take the answer from Step 1, change one of the letters to an R, and get a tooth's anchor:

__ __ __ __ __

Step 3. Take the answer from Step 2, remove two letters, add an A, and get a rodent:

__ __ __ __

Step 4. Take the answer from Step 3, change one of the letters to a C, and get something that chases the answer to Step 3:

___ ___ ___

Step 5. Take the answer from Step 4, insert the letter O, and get something to wear in the cold:

___ ___ ___ ___

Step 6. Take the answer from Step 5, change one of the letters to an L, and get a young horse:

___ ___ ___ ___ ___

Step 7. Take the answer from Step 6, change one letter to an N, change another letter to an I, and get a *COIN!*

Chewed Up Words

Find the letters asked for and place them in order on the teeth. You will spell out three types of teeth. The first one has been done for you.

The first 75% of *inch*
The middle 3 letters of *bison*
the last 2/5 of *alarm*
The first third of *olives*
the middle 3 letters of *march*
The last half of *plus*
The last 60% of *rapid*

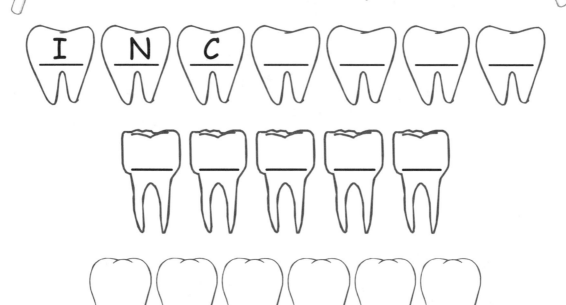

I N C __ __ __ __

__ __ __ __ __

__ __ __ __ __ __

Pillow Search

There are teeth under some of these pillows. Can you help the tooth fairy find the matching pillow for each kid?

Jamie   Bob   Emma   Olivia   Ryan

Pulling Teeth

Untangle the string from each person's tooth and write the correct name in the connected boxes.

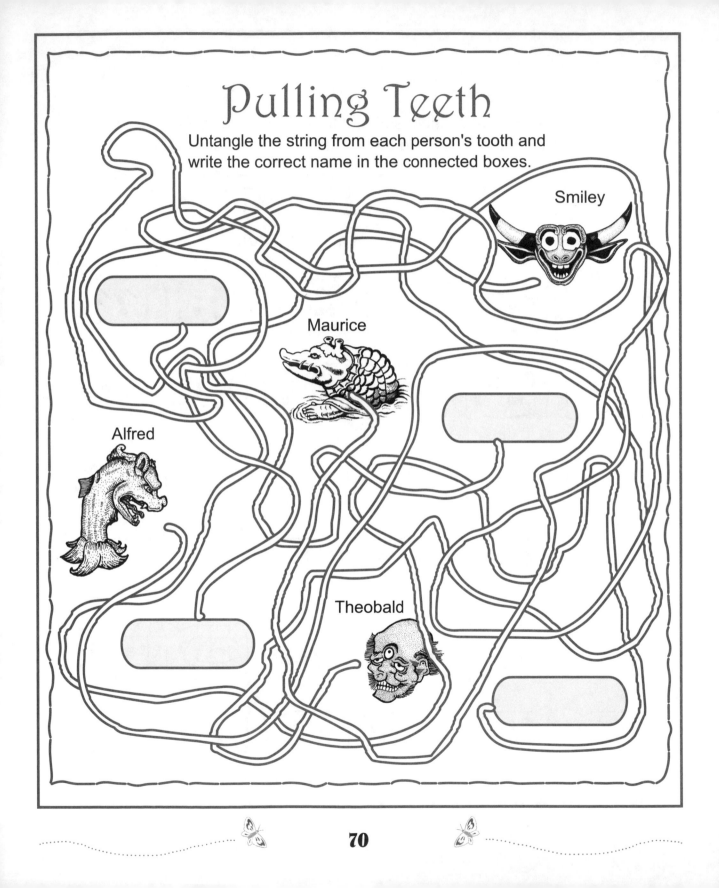

Smiley

Maurice

Alfred

Theobald

Smart Riddle

Answer the clues below and fill the letters into the grid. Work back and forth between the grid and the clues until you figure it out.

A. Horse feet

— — — — —
4   9   17   12   6

B. It gets wetter the more it dries

— — — — —
19   11   13   20   8

C. Found under a tree on a sunny day

— — — — —
15   23   7   16   21

D. A drink made with leaves

— — —
22   3   5

E. Black____: one who works with a hammer and anvil

— — — — —
1   18   14   10   2

Why is the tooth fairy so smart?

1E	2E	3D		4A	5D	6A	
7C		8B	9A	10E		11B	12A
13B	14E	15C	16C	17A	18E		
19B	20B	21C	22D	23C			

Baby teeth are also known as:

____ ____ ____ ____ teeth

Hint: think drink

Tooth Fairy Route

The tooth fairy needs your help finding the quickest route to the house. Stop at the circles and add up all of the numbers along the way. The quickest route will be the path with the lowest total.

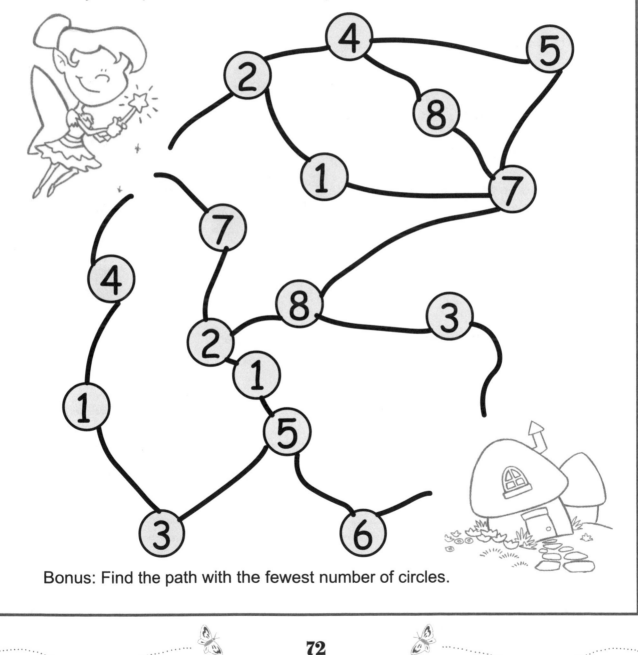

Bonus: Find the path with the fewest number of circles.

Chapter 7

Fairy Friends

Fairy Friend Names

Using the clues below, put the correct name under each fairy friend.

> 1. Dante is between Boris and Kirby.
> 2. Fred is directly below Boris.
> 3. Alex is in the lower-left corner.
> 4. Edgar and Dante are in the same column.

Goblin Numbers

Cross out the one entry in each set that
was added by this mischievous goblin.

5   30
10   17
15
      20
25

$\frac{9}{12}$ .75

$\frac{5}{8}$ $\frac{3}{4}$ $\frac{75}{100}$

75%

4+3
5+4
      2+7
8+1
      3+6
7+1+1

2-2
0+0   15-12-1   12-4-8
      99-99
            14+1-15

4 X 6   3 X 4 X 2
8 X 3
      2 X 12

9-6
      5-2
4-1
            10-7
      7-5
6-3
      5 X 7   6 X 2 X 2

$\frac{3}{15}$ $\frac{25}{100}$
$\frac{1}{5}$
            ?
20% $\frac{5}{25}$

Gremlin's Half Spell

This gremlin accidentally cast a spell that removed half of each of these things. Can you draw the missing halves?

Dwarf Shoppers

Dwarfs are expert miners and very wealthy. Can you figure out what the dwarfs are going to buy with their jewels? Draw a line between each set of jewels and the item with the same value. Here is a guide to the value of each jewel:

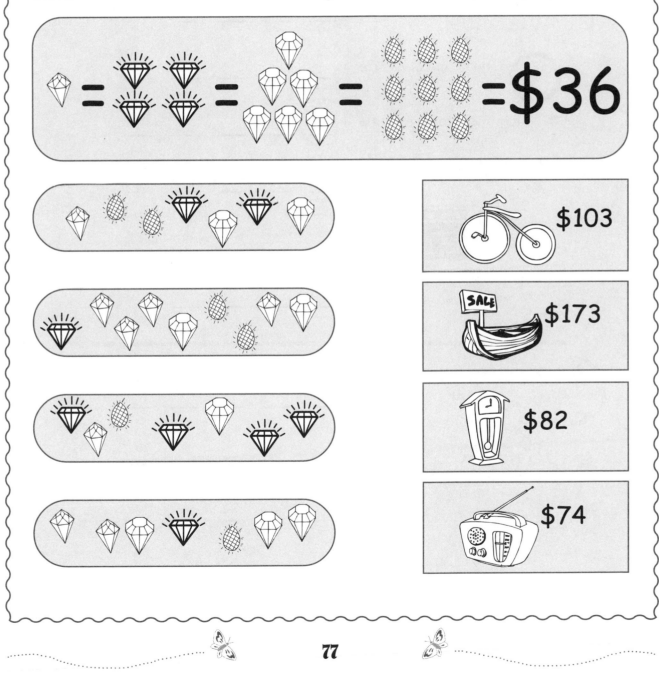

$103

$173

$82

$74

Creature Acrostics

Use the clues and pictures to fill in the blanks. The circled letters will spell the names of creatures that are fairy friends.

Game cubes: ◯ __ __ __

The shape of a circle: ◯ __ __ __ __

It grows into an oak tree: ◯ __ __ __ __

A tropical lizard: ◯ __ __ __ __

It bakes: ◯ __ __ __

It sews: ◯ __ __ __ __ __ __

Our home planet: ◯ __ __ __ __

Joke response: ◯ __ __ __ __

It has petals: ◯ __ __ __ __ __

You can eat lunch on it: ◯ __ __ __ __ __

Water falling: ◯ __ __ __ __

Atlantic or Pacific: ◯ __ __ __ __ __

Found on a tree: ◯ __ __ __ __

It opens with the right key: ◯ __ __ __ __

It fits your hand: ◯ __ __ __ __ __

It smells: ◯ __ __ __ __

Twenty minus nineteen: ◯ __ __ __

Worn on halloween: ◯ __ __ __ __

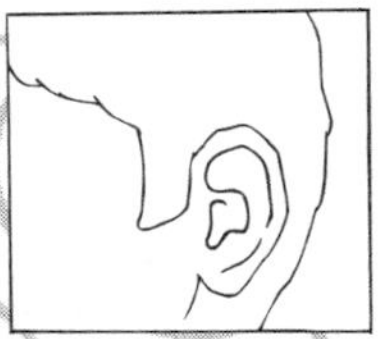

It hears: ◯ __ __ __

20-19

Lucky Four-Leaf Clovers

Leprechauns know that four-leaf clovers are lucky! Can you circle all of the four-leaf clovers on this page? There are twenty of them that look like this:

Elf Cards

Use the clues to determine the correct order for the three Elf cards.

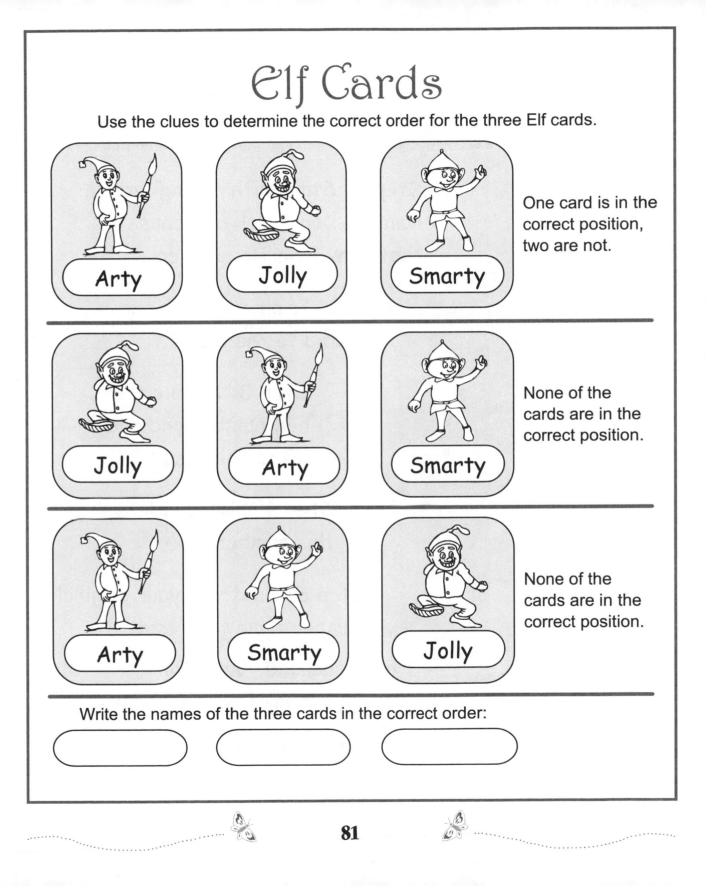

| Arty | Jolly | Smarty | One card is in the correct position, two are not. |

| Jolly | Arty | Smarty | None of the cards are in the correct position. |

| Arty | Smarty | Jolly | None of the cards are in the correct position. |

Write the names of the three cards in the correct order:

Mathmagical Dragon

This dragon can work magic with math. His favorite number is 6. Follow these instructions exactly and he will work magic with your favorite number.

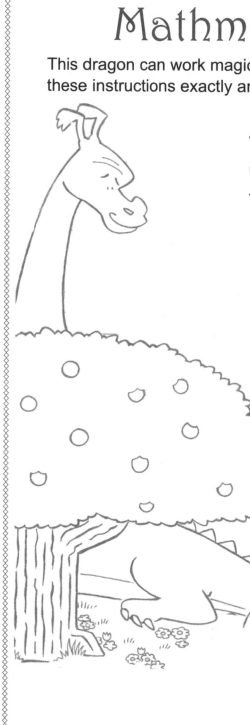

Step 1. Start with your favorite number. Don't pick 6 because that's my favorite number!

Step 2. Triple your number and add 3 to the result.

Step 3. Double that new number and add 30 to the result.

Step 4. Now divide this number by 6.

Step 5. Subtract your original number from the result.

I have changed your favorite number into my favorite number!

How did the mathmagical dragon do this?

Fairy People

Some fairies look just like people. Can you find the fairies on this page? First, draw a line between each description and a person. Then circle the people without a description, they are the fairies!

Graduate   Pilgrim   Chauffeur

Fireman   Janitor

Musician

Doctor

Announcer   Blacksmith

Photographer

Logical Leprechaun

Can you circle the shamrock that comes after the first two?

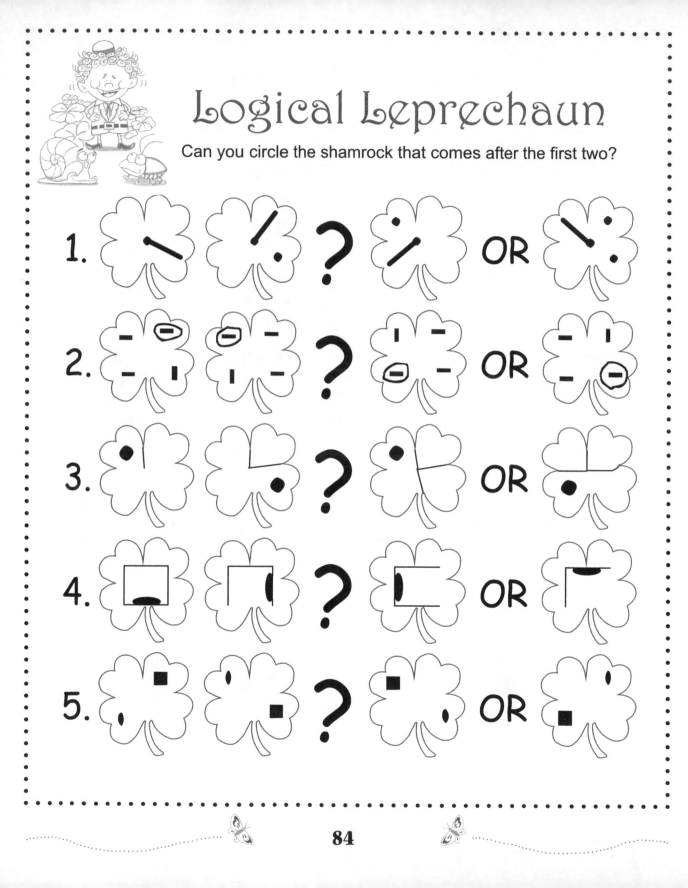

Chapter 8

The Blue Fairy (from "Pinocchio")

Making Pinocchio

The woodcarver Geppetto has 2 hats, 5 shirts, and 3 pants that can fit Pinocchio. How many different combinations of hats, shirts, and pants can Pinocchio wear?

Geppetto's sock drawer is all mixed up! There are 10 black socks, 20 blue socks, and 3 red socks. Without looking at them first, how many socks must Gepetto take out to guarantee that he has a matching pair for Pinocchio?

Help make Pinocchio by drawing his face.

A Heart from the Blue Fairy

Find the heart below that exactly matches the space above for Pinocchio's heart.

Pinocchio's Journey

Help Pinocchio find a path through the woods to the Blue Fairy's castle.

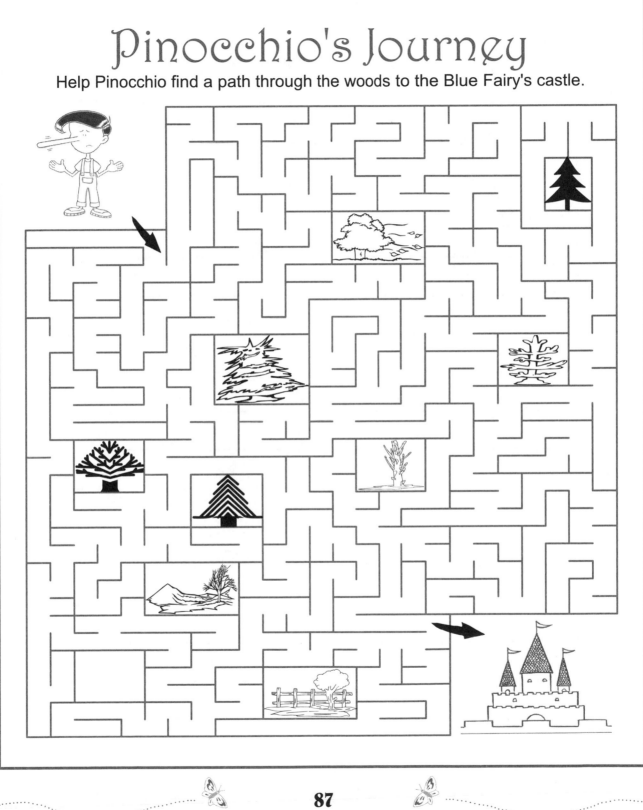

Animal Alphabet

Pinocchio sold his school book so that he could buy a ticket to the puppet show! The Blue Fairy needs your help to teach the alphabet to Pinocchio. Write the name of an animal that begins with each letter below. Some of the letters already have animals.

A_____

B_____

C_____

D_____

E_____

F_____

G_____

H_____

I_____

J_____

K_____

L_____

M_____

Newt_____

O_____

P_____

Q_____

R_____

S_____

T_____

Urchin_____

Vulture_____

W_____

Xenops_____

Yak_____

Z_____

Puppet Shows

Pinocchio saw his brothers and sisters on the stage.
Can you find ten differences between these two shows?

Candy Counter

Pinocchio went to the land of toys where boys play all day and eat only candy. Use the clues to figure out how many pieces of candy each boy has.

Steve has fewer pieces than Pinocchio, but more pieces than Frank.

Frank has as many pieces as Justin and Ray combined.

Justin has twice the number of pieces as Ray.

The Blue Fairy says that Pinocchio has 5 pieces of candy.

Pinocchio has 3 more pieces than Justin.

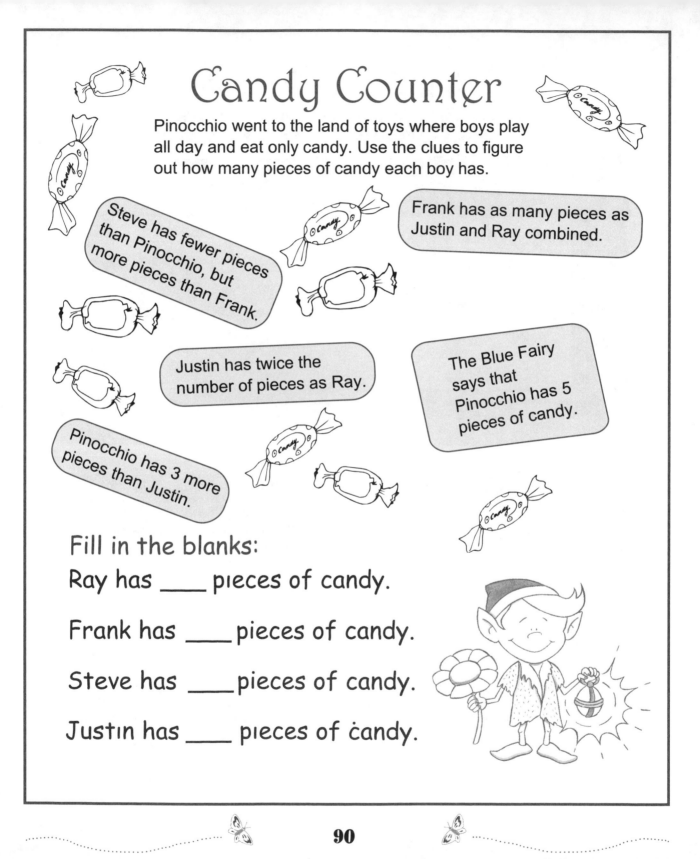

Fill in the blanks:

Ray has ____ pieces of candy.

Frank has ____ pieces of candy.

Steve has ____ pieces of candy.

Justin has ____ pieces of candy.

Magic Squares

The Blue Fairy is using magic squares to teach Pinocchio about math. Here is an example of a magic square:

2	9	4
7	5	3
6	1	8

A 3x3 magic square has these properties:
1. Each number from 1 to 9 is used once.
2. The sum of each row, column, and diagonal is the same.

Complete these magic squares by putting numbers into the empty boxes:

4	3	8
	5	
2		6

	1	6
	5	7
	4	

6		2
		9
	3	

6		
	5	
		4

Can you complete these 4x4 magic squares? They are just like 3x3 magic squares, except the numbers 1 to 16 are used.

16	3		13
5		11	8
9	6	7	12
	15	14	

4		9	
	10		3
	11	7	
1	8	12	13

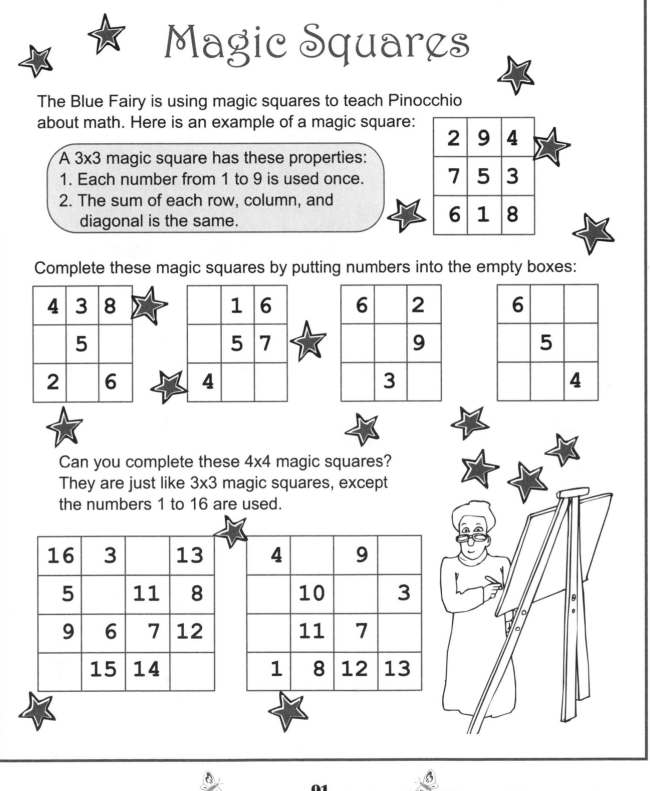

91

The Field of Wonders

Pinocchio foolishly tried to grow his money by planting it in the field of wonders. Follow the clues to help the Blue Fairy figure out where Pinocchio buried his money.

Pinocchio buried his money under a flower that...
1. ...is in a column that has more than 2 digits.
2. ...has a number in the square directly below it.
3. ...is in a row where the digits add up to 26.
4. ...is not in a column that has a repeated digit.

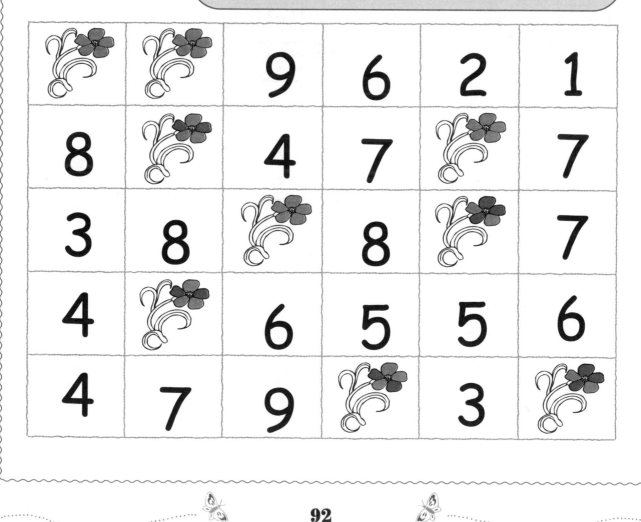

Tell the Truth

Pinocchio's nose grew when he lied to the Blue Fairy about what happened to his money. Circle the kids on this page who are telling the truth.

Andrew has 38¢
"The boys have more money than the girls."

Olivia has 76¢
"All of the kids together have a total of $3.36"

Matthew has 62¢
"Emma has more money than Andrew and Jacob combined."

Samantha has 25¢
"The kids with 6 letters in their names have a total of $1.14"

Jacob has 47¢
"All combined, the girls have an even number of cents."

Emma has 88¢
"The person with the least amount of money is a boy."

How much does a school lunch cost if Emma has exactly enough money to buy one every day from Tuesday through Friday?

Fishing for Father

Pinocchio is looking for his father who is inside a fish sitting at a table with a candle! Find the fish that has all of the letters in these words: GEPPETTO, TABLE, CHAIR, CANDLE.

Back to the Blue Fairy

After rescuing his father from the fish, Pinocchio must swim back to the Blue Fairy. A shark gives him these directions: *"Swim 1 mile north, 2 miles east, 3 miles south, 2 miles west and you will find land."* **Can you find a shorter route?**

Changes

The Blue Fairy helped Pinocchio change from a puppet into a real boy. Can you change one word into another word in these puzzles? Each step must be a real word and differ from the previous word by only one letter. There are many possible solutions, but try to use only the given number of steps.

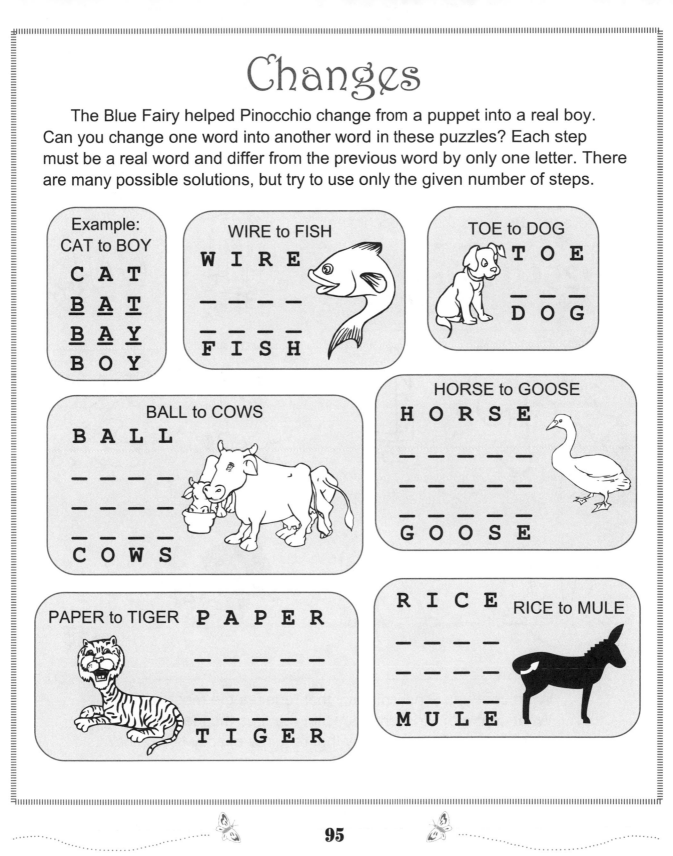

Example: CAT to BOY

C A T
<u>B</u> <u>A</u> T
<u>B</u> A <u>Y</u>
B O Y

WIRE to FISH

W I R E
_ _ _ _
_ _ _ _
F I S H

TOE to DOG

T O E
_ _ _
_ _ _
D O G

BALL to COWS

B A L L
_ _ _ _
_ _ _ _
C O W S

HORSE to GOOSE

H O R S E
_ _ _ _ _
_ _ _ _ _
G O O S E

PAPER to TIGER

P A P E R
_ _ _ _ _
_ _ _ _ _
T I G E R

RICE to MULE

R I C E
_ _ _ _
_ _ _ _
M U L E

Geppetto's New Coat

With the help of the Blue Fairy, Pinocchio has earned enough money to buy Geppetto a new coat. Exact change must be used to buy the coats on this page. Circle the coats that Pinocchio can buy.

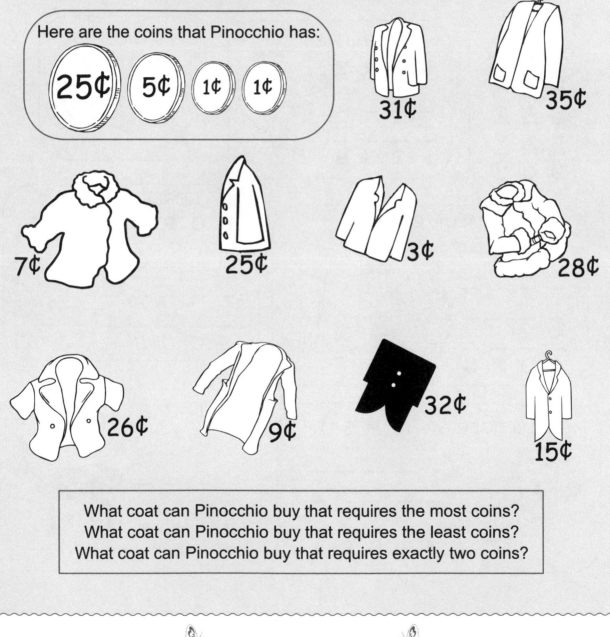

Here are the coins that Pinocchio has:

25¢   5¢   1¢   1¢

31¢

35¢

7¢

25¢

3¢

28¢

26¢

9¢

32¢

15¢

What coat can Pinocchio buy that requires the most coins?
What coat can Pinocchio buy that requires the least coins?
What coat can Pinocchio buy that requires exactly two coins?

Chapter 9

Thumbelina

Magic Seeds

Thumbelina grew like magic from a seed! Draw magic seeds into the empty squares to complete the four garden plots. There are four magic seeds:

heart   diamond   triangle   square

Within every plot, each seed should appear only once in each row, column, and 2x2 box.

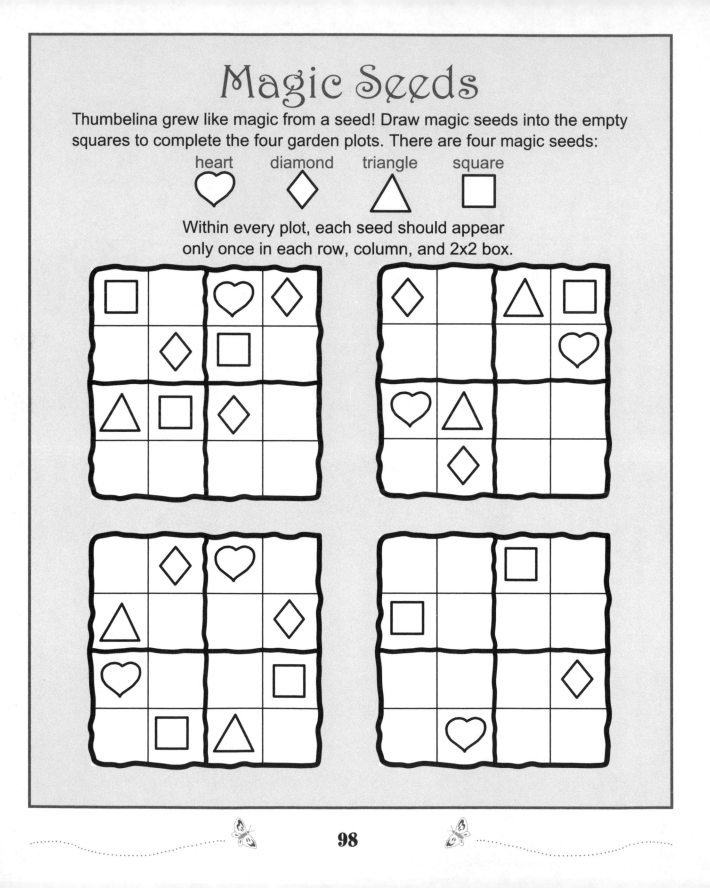

Thumbelina's Country

To find out the country where *Thumbelina* was written, first put a letter in each box that corresponds to the starting letter of the pictures. Then, unscramble the letters to form the name of a country.

_ _ _ _ _ _ _

Memories

Try to remember all of the details of things you see on this page. Then turn to the next page and see if you can answer some true-false questions from memory.

Don't read this until you have looked at the previous page!

STOP

Memories

After carefully studying the previous page, see if you can answer each of these questions either TRUE or FALSE. No peeking!

_____ There is a paddle with the kayak.

_____ The egg is decorated.

_____ There is an earring on the ear.

_____ There is a ribbon through a nine.

_____ The rug is laid out completely flat.

_____ The dog is standing on one leg.

_____ The arrow is pointing up.

_____ There is a key.

_____ The apple does not have a stem.

_____ There is a horse with a saddle.

_____ The nuts have a shell.

_____ The rope is in a loop.

_____ There are eight groups of pictures.

_____ The needle is threaded.

_____ The magnet has a triangle shape.

Author

Decode the numbers below to find out the author of *Thumbelina*. 1=A, 2=B, 3=C, etc.

8___

1___

14___

19___

1___

14___

3___

8___

4___

18___

5___

9___

18___

19___

19___

5___

20___

14___

9___

1___

14___

Butterfly Friends

Thumbelina was helped by a butterfly who pulled her to safety. Help these butterflies find their way home by drawing a line from each butterfly to a corresponding flower. Can you figure out the pattern that connects each butterfly to a flower? One pair has already been matched.

Hint: Multiply the digits on each butterfly and add the digits on each flower.

Falling Leaves

All summer long, Thumbelina lived happily in the forest.
When Fall came, the weather grew cold and the leaves fell.
Draw a line from each piece to its place in the picture.

Mouse House Route

When winter came, Thumbelina stayed in the house of a mouse.
Can you trace Thumbelina's route? She covered all the dashed
lines and did not cross over or go back along any line.

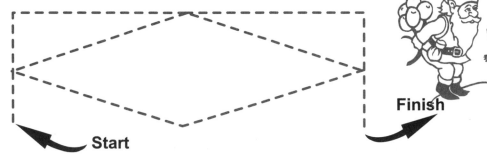

Start

Finish

Escape from Mr. Mole

Help Thumbelina find a path from Mr. Mole to the bird.
The bird will help Thumbelina escape.

Carrots and Apples

Thumbelina started her journey to fairyland with no food in her bag! She made four stops along the way...

1 Thumbelina stopped at a lake and found three carrots. She ate one of the carrots and took the rest in her bag to the next stop...

2 Thumbelina stopped at a tree house and found five apples. She ate two of them and took the rest in her bag to the next stop...

3 Thumbelina stopped at a farm and found four more carrots and three more apples. She ate three carrots and one apple and took the rest in her bag to the next stop...

4 Thumbelina stopped at a castle and ate two carrots and two apples from her bag and took the rest to fairyland.

How many carrots and apples did Thumbelina have in her bag after each stop?

	Carrots	Apples
Lake		
Tree House		
Farm		
Castle		

Many Emotions

Thumbelina has all kinds of experiences.
Draw her face to express these emotions...

Surprised when she was kidnapped by the frogs.

Sad when she almost had to marry Mr. Mole.

Happy when she marries the fairy prince.

Dress Up

Thumbelina loves to dress up her friends in fairyland.
Color these friends so they each have a unique dress...

Thumbelina's Crossword

In honor of Thumbelina's arrival in fairyland, the fairy prince made this crossword puzzle. The words use only letters from her name: THUMBELINA.

ACROSS

4 You have a first, middle, and last one
5 Opposite of fat
6 To search for prey
9 A being from outer space
11 Scientists' workplace
12 Green citrus fruit
13 Clue for the stumped
14 A sad color
17 Hamburger bread
18 There are 60 in an hour
19 Part of a dog that wags
20 Mary had a little one
22 Connects two points
24 Furnace output
26 After dinner candy and toothpaste flavor
28 Breakfast, lunch, or dinner
30 Fish that comes in a can
31 Between nine and eleven

DOWN

1 The science of numbers and their operations
2 Not nice
3 A female adult chicken
5 A blue-green color
7 Furniture piece with legs
8 Balloon gas
10 Read when seated at a restaurant
15 Opposite of early
16 Your mother's sister
17 It holds pants up.
21 Delivered daily to your box
22 A fib
23 It is hit with a hammer
25 What you do at a restaurant
27 Clean and tidy
29 Worn on the head
32 Acorn and almond, for example

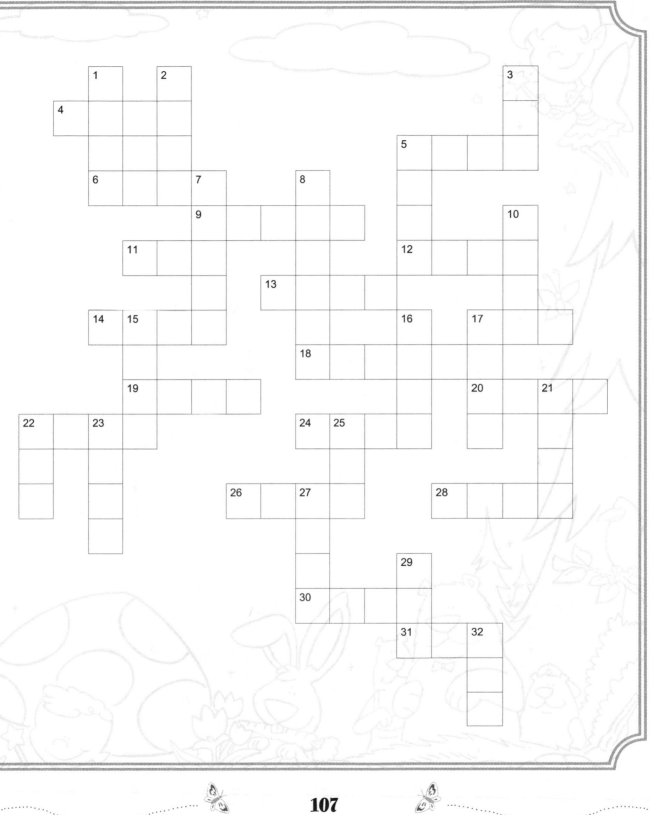

Wedding Invitation Lists

Thumbelina and the fairy prince need your help to complete their wedding invitation lists. Each list has a certain type of name. For example, one list is just for names that include the letter Z. Draw a line from each name to the list it belongs to, and give a reason why.

Reese

Hazel

Jason

Eve

Charlotte

Brook
Isaac
Aaron
Kaylee
Ashlee

Ava
Hannah
Bob
Harrah
Okonoko

Matthew
Garrett
Scott
Brittany
Juliette

Madison
Sonia
Carson
Sonny
Garrison

Elizabeth
Zachary
ZhiRong
Mackenzie
Zane

Inhabitants of Fairyland

Here are some of the mythical creatures that exist in fairyland.

Leprechauns
These fairy friends come from Ireland and are known to be rather sly and tricky. They are also filthy rich and keep pots of gold hidden just out of view.

Goblins
These fairy creatures are mischievous villains who are not to be trusted! They are very smart and nearly invisible.

Dwarfs
Fairy creatures who are small yet excellent warriors, dwarfs prefer to live underground and are known to be able to see in the dark.

Pixies
You might catch a glimpse of these tiny fairy creatures dancing in the shadows. They are fun-loving and hard-working, and sometimes steal horses!

Giants
Known for their enormous size and strength, giants are frequently in conflict with the gods in various stories. They are not especially intelligent or friendly.

Mermaids
Beautiful sea creatures who are half-human and half-fish, mermaids love to comb their long hair and admire their reflection in the water.

Unicorns
This fairyland creature looks like a horse except for the horn on its forehead. Legend has it that a unicorn's horn has the ability to neutralize poison.

Gnomes
These fairyland friends appear as very small men, usually with white beards and tall pointed caps. Gnomes are frequently seen in gardens.

Dragons
Reptile creatures of the fairy world, dragons look a bit like large lizards. Dragons can be quite friendly, though they are often feared.

Elves
These fairyland beings love natural places like forests. They appear as youthful men and women with great beauty and are thought to be immortal.

Griffin
One of the most powerful and majestic of all the creatures in fairyland, griffins have the body of a lion and the head and wings of an eagle.

Appendix B
Fun Web Sites

www.fairychildren.com
Fairy fun for children of all ages. Includes pages to print and color.

www.funster.com
Compete against friends at this Web site with multiplayer word games and other puzzles. Created by the author of this book!

www.disneyfairies.com
Meet all of your favorite fairies here. Filled with numerous games and activities.

www.funschool.com
The emphasis is definitely on fun at this Web site with a variety of games for every grade.

www.allaboutunicorns.com
Everything you need to know about unicorns and their history. Includes pretty pictures of unicorns.

www.funbrain.com
Loaded with brainy (but really fun) games for kids of all ages.

www.i-dressup.com
For those in love with fashion, style, and dress up games!

www.toothfairy.org
All about the tooth fairy and how to take care of your teeth.

www.bonus.com
Chock-full of fun games of all types. Check out the Family section that includes Arts & Crafts.

www.fairiesworld.com
An online encyclopedia about fairies filled with information and illustrations.

Appendix C
Puzzle Answers

Page vi • Find the Pictures

Page 3 • Butterfly Twins

Page 2 • The Path to Fairyland

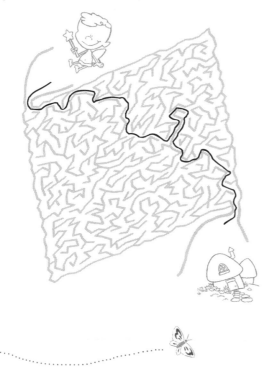

Page 4 • Fairyland Photos

Page 5 • **Fairy Foods**

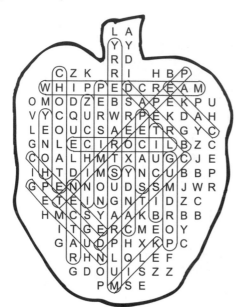

Page 7 • **Fairyland Code**

ALL THINGS ARE POSSIBLE IN FAIRYLAND!

Page 6 • **Fairy Hill**

Page 8 • **Fairyland Plants & Animals**

1) BUMBLEBEE
2) BUTTERFLY
3) DUCK
4) FLOWER
5) FROG
6) MUSHROOM
7) SNAIL
8) BIRD
9) RACCOON
10) TREE

Page 9 • Fairyland Plants & Animals

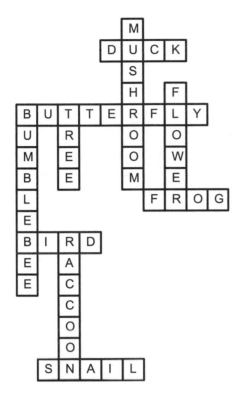

Page 11 • Triangle Mushrooms

Page 10 • The Language of Fairyland

A playground for a toothy ocean animal is a:
SHARK PARK

A rodent abode is a:
MOUSE HOUSE

A birthday treat for a scaly friend is a:
SNAKE CAKE

A utensil to eat a dried plum is a:
PRUNE SPOON

Page 12 • Fairyland Riddles

Page 14 • **Directions Home**

D) U, R, R, D, R, R, U, U, U, L, L, U

Page 15 • **Fairy Dust Letters**

PORCUPINE	GERBIL
LEOPARD	CHEETAH
HORSE	CHIPMUNK
RHINOCEROS	JAGUAR
RACCOON	HEDGEHOG
ZEBRA	HAMSTER
RABBIT	HIPPOPOTAMUS
ELEPHANT	TIGER
GIRAFFE	DOLPHIN
CAMEL	COYOTE

Page 17 • **Magical Changes**

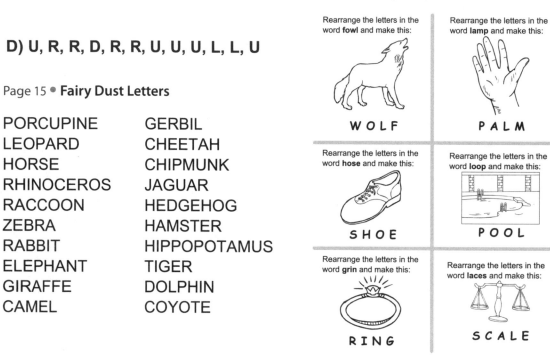

Rearrange the letters in the word **fowl** and make this:

W O L F

Rearrange the letters in the word **lamp** and make this:

P A L M

Rearrange the letters in the word **hose** and make this:

S H O E

Rearrange the letters in the word **loop** and make this:

P O O L

Rearrange the letters in the word **grin** and make this:

R I N G

Rearrange the letters in the word **laces** and make this:

S C A L E

Page 16 • **Magical Changes**

Rearrange the letters in the word **gum** and make this:

M U G

Rearrange the letters in the word **art** and make this:

R A T

Rearrange the letters in the word **disk** and make these:

K I D S

Rearrange the letters in the word **flea** and make this:

L E A F

Page 18 • **Whose Wand?**

Page 19 • **Break the Spell**

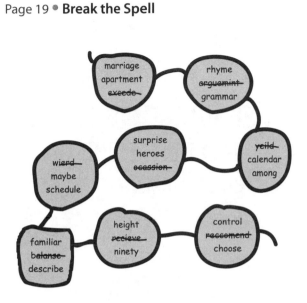

Page 21 • **Cinderella's Magic Time**

Page 20 • **Cinderella's Glass Slipper**

Page 22 • **Riddles**

Why is six afraid of seven?
Because seven eight nine!

What clothing does a house wear?
Address!

What is in the middle of Paris?
The letter R!

What happens when an egg laughs?
It cracks up!

What month has 28 days?
All of them!

What has four legs but only one foot?
A bed!

  115

Page 24 • **What's Next?**

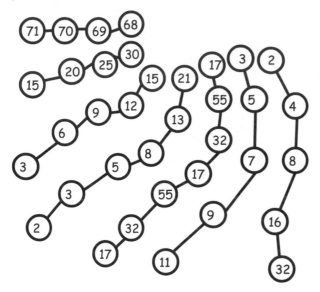

Page 27 • **A Flower Fairy Christmas**

POINSETTIA

Page 27 • **Flowery Dividers**

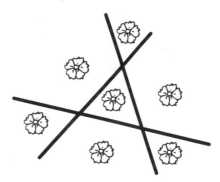

Page 26 • **Flower Maze**

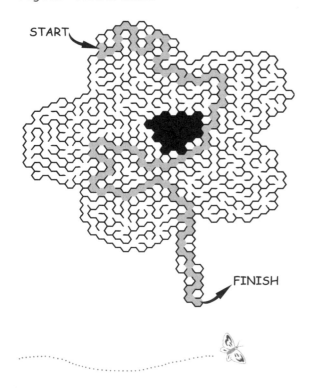

START

FINISH

Page 28 • **Flower Values**

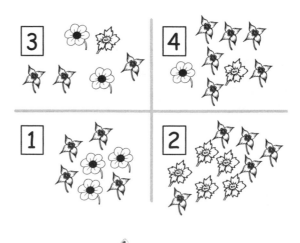

Page 29 • **The Flower Fairy Garden**

1. WATER
2. CORN
3. HOE
4. BUGS
5. SEEDS
6. TOPSOIL
7. NOSE

Page 31 • **Ower Words**

SNOW BLOWER

ROWER

TOWER

SHOWER

LAWN MOWER

Page 30 • **Smart Shopper**

Daisies
1 dozen for $18 ($1.50 each, **best buy!**)
5 for $8 ($1.60 each)

Marigolds
$2.75 each (**best buy!**)
OR
5 for $14 ($2.80 each)

Roses
7 for $7.70 ($1.10 each)
OR
20 for $21 ($1.05 each, **best buy!**)

Tulips
half dozen for $9 ($1.50 each, **best buy!**)
OR
2 for $3.50 ($1.75 each)

Carnations
8 for $10 ($1.25 each)
OR
3 for $3.45 ($1.15 each, **best buy!**)

The **roses** are the cheapest flower of all.

Page 32 • **Flower Riddles**

A. Vegetable found in a pod.

P E A
17 18 20

B. What do you do on a chair?

S I T
16 14 9

C. A place for coats.

C L O S E T
3 21 11 12 2 19

D. Something with four legs.

T A B L E
13 4 1 10 7

E. Clubs, diamonds, hearts, and spades.

S U I T S
6 5 8 15 22

1D	2C	3C	4D	5E	6E	7D		8E	9B
B	E	C	A	U	S	E		I	T
10D	**11C**	**12C**	**13D**		**14B**	**15E**	**16B**		
L	O	S	T		I	T	S		
17A	**18A**	**19C**	**20A**	**21C**	**22E**				
P	E	T	A	L	S	!			

If April showers bring May flowers, what do May flowers bring? **Pilgrims**

Page 33 • **Flower Equations**

Page 35 • **Flower Fairy Delivery**

Page 34 • **Flowery Search**

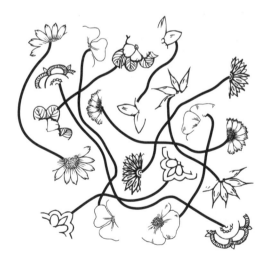

Page 36 • **Fractured Flowers**

Pages 38-39 • **Antique Books**

Page 40 • **Three Bears' Bingo**

17 + 3 = 20
11 + 11 = 22
11 + 17 + 8 = 36
9 + 8 + 7 = 24
33 + 28 + 33 = 94
82 - 4 = 78
93 - 9 = 84
78 - 11 = 67
56 ÷ 8 = 7
10 X 5 = 50
5 X 9 = 45
34 ÷ 2 = 17
26 ÷ 13 = 2
4 X 11 = 44
90 ÷ 9 = 10
27 - 8 = 19
10 + 20 + 7 = 37
25 ÷ 5 = 5
37 - 26 = 11
2 X 7 = 14

Mama Bear wins!

Page 41 • **Rapunzel's Hair Connection**

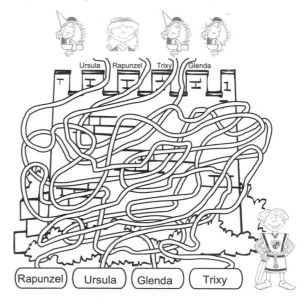

Page 42 • **Mother Goose Words**

Here are some of the words that can be made with the letters in MOTHER GOOSE:

gee, gem, germ, get, ghost, go, gore, gosh, got, greet, groom, he, her, here, hero, hoe, hog, horse, hose, host, hot, me, meet, mere, mesh, met, meter, moose, more, most, moth, motor, oh, or, ore, other, remote, reset, rest, room, roost, root, rot, see, seem, set, she, sheet, shoe, shoot, shore, short, shot, smooth, so, some, sore, sort, steer, stem, store, storm, tee, teem, term, the, them, theme, there, these, those, three, to, toe, too, tore, tree

You might have found others. More words can be made by adding letters to these words.

Page 43 • **The Prince's Real Clothes**

Page 44 • **Hansel & Gretel**

Page 45 • **The Gingerbread House**

Page 46 • **The Three Little Pigs**

971 Haystack St

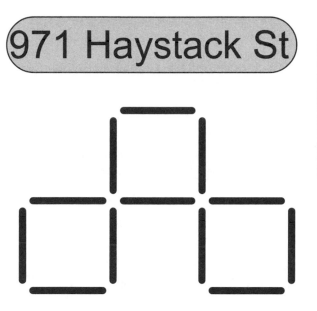

6,000 bricks are needed.
(2 X 10 X 300 = 6,000)

Page 47 • **The Princess and the Pea**

PEACE

PEACH

PEACOCK

SPEAR

PEAR

PEARL

PEANUT

Page 48 • **Wedding Bells**

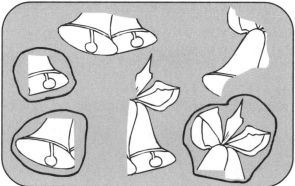

Page 48 • **The End. . .**

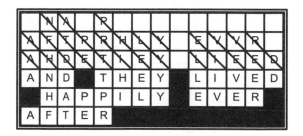

Page 50 • Latin Unicorn

one wheel: UNICYCLE
one outfit: UNIFORM
together as one: UNITED
one sound: UNISON

a type of horn: CORNUCOPIA

Page 51 • Secret Message

If you'll believe in me, I'll believe in you.

Page 51 • Unicorn Healers

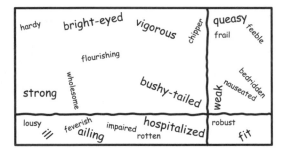

Page 52 • Horse Barn

Page 53 • Hidden Horns

Rather than have a big wedding, the eleph**ant elope**d with his bride. (antelope)

The melodi**c ow**l played trumpet in the band. (cow)

The monkey ate a man**go at**op the house. (goat)

Suzy has been a film **buff a lo**ng time and loves romantic comedies. (buffalo)

Page 53 • Be a Deer

A deer's horns are called **_antlers_**. They are made of **_bone_** and are shed and regrown each **_year_**.

Pages 54-55 • **The Unicorn Trio**

Ullric

4:03

Ulysses

4:18

Umberto

4:23

The unicorn with three repeated letters in his name will deliver a letter for the princess. Who is it?

Ulysses

The unicorn whose name has all the letters in the word **TURBO** will pull the princess's carriage. Who is it?

Umberto

An even number of letters is in the name of the unicorn who will find a lost lamb for the princess. Who is it?

Ullric

Page 55 • **Lunch Time!**

Ullric   Umberto   Ulysses

Page 55 • **Better Barns**

Ullric   Umberto   Ulysses

Page 56 • **Shadow of a Unicorn**

Page 56 • **Unicorn Twin**

Page 57 • **Maiden's Song**

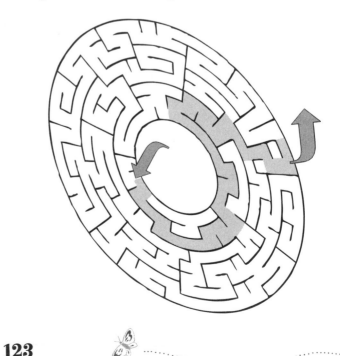

123

Page 58 • **Portrait of a Unicorn**

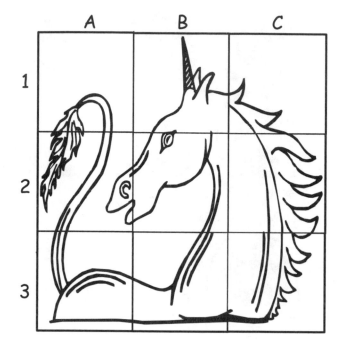

Page 60 • **Going Up**

2	31	64	79	75	94	37	69	19	72	99
22	6	66	56	45	55	67	43	45	54	96
86	34	76	62	66	67	73	75	77	87	90
80	31	75	60	19	81	59	96	94	86	84
48	35	65	55	53	50	36	18	10	92	50
22	33	31	61	60	49	71	14	84	30	69
11	91	66	42	85	45	44	43	41	39	81
10	97	51	33	85	10	40	55	70	38	87
9	15	19	22	25	54	54	16	25	36	72
7	20	25	33	28	29	30	31	33	35	71
1	21	19	45	47	55	56	57	59	63	65

Puzzle Answers

Page 62 • Tooth Fairy Animal

$$\underset{1}{M} \quad \underset{2}{O} \quad \underset{3}{U} \quad \underset{4}{S} \quad \underset{5}{E}$$

Page 62 • Baby Teeth

```
   3 number of colors in the U.S. flag
-  2 number of cups in a pint
+ 60 number of seconds in a minute
-  4 even number between 2 and 5
- 25 number of cents in a quarter
- 12 number of inches in a foot
―――――――――――――――――――――――――――
= 20 total number of baby teeth
```

Page 63 • A Healthy Smile

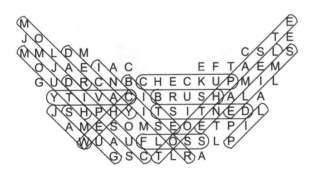

Page 64 • Sweet Tooth

Page 65 • A Good Deal

25 cents X 8 teeth = $2.00

$.01 + $.02 + $.04 + $.08 + $.16 + $.32
+ $.64 + $1.28 = **$2.55, the best deal!**

Page 65 • Fast Fairy

7 minutes X 19 teeth = 133 minutes
133 minutes = 2 hours 13 minutes
11:24 p.m. + 2 hours 13 minutes =
1:37 a.m.

Page 66 • Step by Step

Step 1: TOOT
Step 2: ROOT
Step 3: RAT
Step 4: CAT
Step 5: COAT
Step 6: COLT
Step 7: COIN

Page 68 • Chewed Up Words

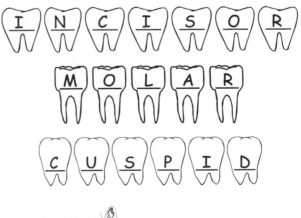

Page 69 • Pillow Search

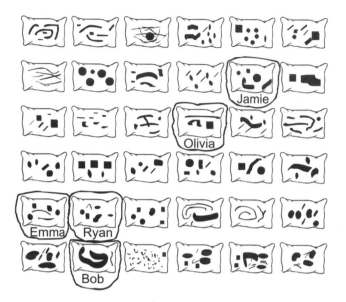

Page 70 • Pulling Teeth

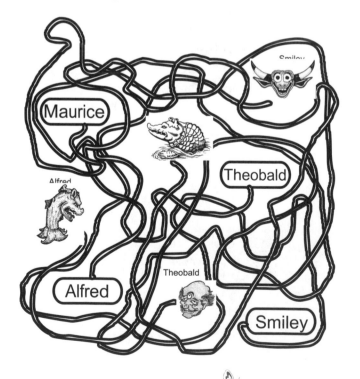

Page 71 • Smart Riddle

A. Horse feet

H O O F S
4 9 17 12 6

B. It gets wetter the more it dries

T O W E L
19 11 13 20 8

C. Found under a tree on a sunny day

S H A D E
15 23 7 16 21

D. A drink made with leaves

T E A
22 3 5

E. Black____: one who works with a hammer and anvil

S M I T H
1 18 14 10 2

1E	2E	3D		4A	5D	6A	
S	H	E		H	A	S	
7C		8B	9A	10E		11B	12A
A		L	O	T		O	F
13B	14E	15C	16C	17A	18E		
W	I	S	D	O	M		
19B	20B	21C	22D	23C			
T	E	E	T	H			

Baby teeth are also known as:
MILK teeth

Page 72 • **Tooth Fairy Route**

Page 74 • **Fairy Friend**

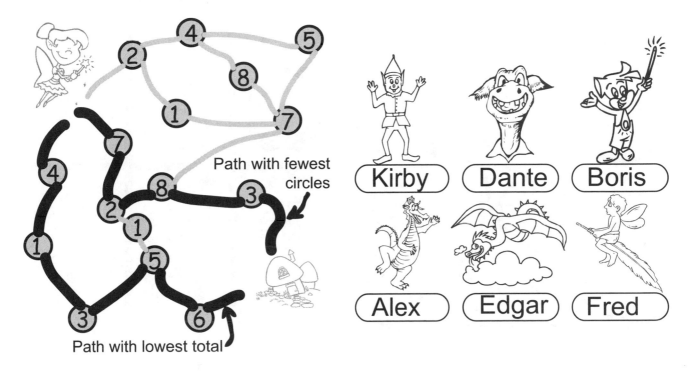

Path with fewest circles

Path with lowest total

Kirby   Dante   Boris

Alex   Edgar   Fred

Page 75 • Goblin Numbers

Page 76 • Gremlin's Half Spell

Page 77 • Dwarf Shoppers

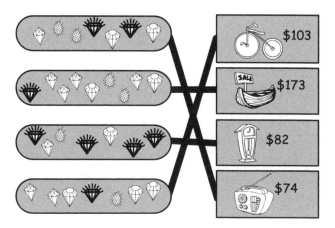

Page 78 • **Creature Acrostics**

(D) I C E
(R) O U N D
(A) C O R N
(G) E C K O
(O) V E N
(N) E E D L E

(E) A R T H
(L) A U G H
(F) L O W E R

(T) A B L E
(R) A I N
(O) C E A N
(L) E A F
(L) O C K

(G) L O V E
(N) O S E
(O) N E
(M) A S K
(E) A R

Page 80 • **Lucky Four-Leaf Clovers**

Page 81 • **Elf Cards**

(Smarty) (Jolly) (Arty)

Page 82 • **Mathmagical Dragon**

This explanation uses algebra:
Step 1. n = your number
Step 2. 3n + 3
Step 3. 2(3n + 3) + 30 = 6n + 36
Step 4. (6n + 36)/6 = n + 6
Step 5. n + 6 — n = 6

Page 83 • **Fairy People**

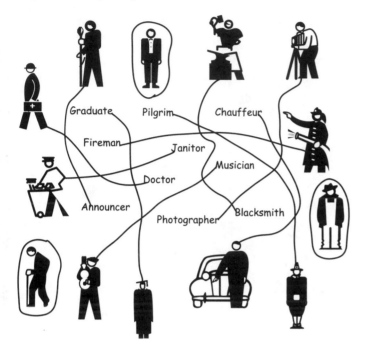

Page 84 • **Logical Leprechaun**

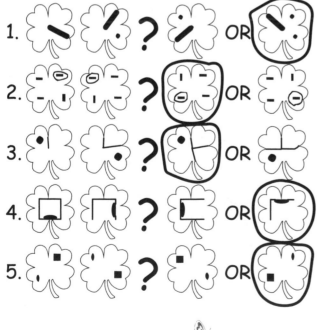

Page 86 • Making Pinochio

2 hats X 5 shirts X 3 pants = **30** combinations of hats, shirts, and pants.

Gepetto must take out **4** socks from the drawer to guarantee that at least two of them match.

Page 86 • A Heart from the Blue Fairy

Page 87 • Pinochio's Journey

Page 88 • Animal Alphabet

Here are some answers for this puzzle. You may have found others.

A Animals: Aardvark Alligator Ape

B Animals: Baboon Bat Bear Beaver Bird Bunny

C Animals: Camel Cat Chameleon Cheetah Chicken Cow Coyote Crab Crocodile

D Animals: Deer Dog Dolphin Donkey Duck

E Animals: Eagle Eel Elephant

F Animals: Falcon Fish Flamingo Fox Frog

G Animals: Gazelle Gecko Giraffe Goat Goose Gorilla Groundhog Guinea Pig

H Animals: Hen Hippopotamus Horse

I Animals: Iguana

J Animals: Jackal Jaguar Jellyfish

K Animals: Kangaroo Kiwi Koala Bear Kookaburra

L Animals: Lamb Leopard Lion Lizard Llama Lobster

M Animals: Monkey Moose Mouse

O Animals: Octopus Orangutan Ostrich Owl Ox

P Animals: Panda Panther Parrot Penguin Pig

Q Animals: Quail

R Animals: Rabbit Raccoon Rattlesnake Rhinoceros

S Animals: Seal Shark Sheep Skunk Snake Squirrel

T Animals: Tiger Tortoise Turkey Turtle

W Animals: Walrus Weasel Whale Wolf

Z Animals: Zebra

Page 89 • **Puppet Shows**

Page 91 • **Magic Squares**

4	3	8
9	5	1
2	7	6

8	1	6
3	5	7
4	9	2

6	7	2
1	5	9
8	3	4

6	1	8
7	5	3
2	9	4

16	3	2	13
5	10	11	8
9	6	7	12
4	15	14	1

4	5	9	16
15	10	6	3
14	11	7	2
1	8	12	13

Page 90 • **Candy Counter**

Ray has __1__ pieces of candy.

Frank has __3__ pieces of candy.

Steve has __4__ pieces of candy.

Justin has __2__ pieces of candy.

Page 92 • **The Field of Wonders**

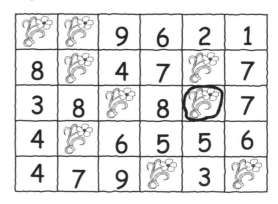

Page 93 • **Tell the Truth**

Andrew has 38¢
"The boys have more money than the girls."

Olivia has 76¢
"All of the kids together have a total of $3.36"

Matthew has 62¢
"Emma has more money than Andrew and Jacob combined."

Samantha has 25¢
"The kids with 6 letters in their names have a total of $1.14"

Jacob has 47¢
"All combined, the girls have an even number of cents."

Emma has 88¢
"The person with the least amount of money is a boy."

A school lunch costs 22¢

Page 94 • **Fishing for Father**

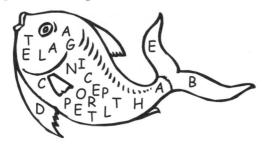

Page 94 • **Back to the Blue Fairy**

Pinocchio just needs to swim 2 miles south to find land.

Page 95 • **Changes**

There are many possible solutions. Here are our answers:

WIRE	TOE
WISE	DOE
WISH	DOG
FISH	
	HORSE
BALL	HOUSE
BAWL	MOUSE
BOWL	MOOSE
BOWS	GOOSE
COWS	
	RICE
PAPER	RIDE
TAPER	RUDE
TAMER	RULE
TIMER	MULE
TIGER	

Page 96 • **Geppetto's New Coat**

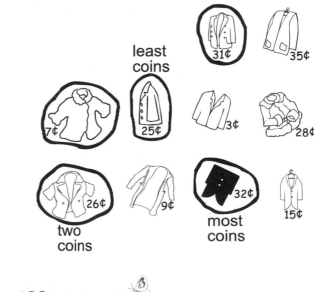

least coins

31¢ 35¢

7¢ 25¢ 3¢ 28¢

two coins 26¢ 9¢ 32¢ most coins 15¢

Page 98 • **Magic Seeds**

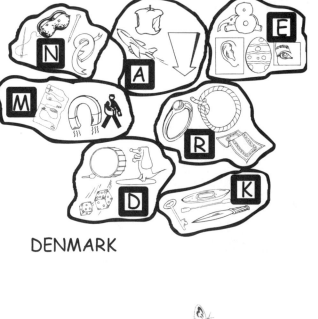

Page 99 • **Thumbelina's Country**

DENMARK

Page 100 • **Memories**

__TRUE__ There is a paddle with the kayak.

__TRUE__ The egg is decorated.

__FALSE__ There is an earring on the ear.

__TRUE__ There is a ribbon through a nine.

__FALSE__ The rug is laid out completely flat.

__FALSE__ The dog is standing on one leg.

__FALSE__ The arrow is pointing up.

__TRUE__ There is a key.

__FALSE__ The apple does not have a stem.

__FALSE__ There is a horse with a saddle.

__TRUE__ The nuts have a shell.

__TRUE__ The rope is in a loop.

__FALSE__ There are eight groups of pictures.

__TRUE__ The needle is threaded.

__FALSE__ The magnet has a triangle shape.

Page 100 • **Author**

8 H
1 A
14 N
19 S

3 C
8 H
18 R
9 I
19 S
20 T
9 I
1 A
14 N

1 A
14 N
4 D
5 E
18 R
19 S
5 E
14 N

Page 101 • **Butterfly Friends**

The digits on a butterfly
multiplied should equal the
sum of the digits on a flower.

Page 102 • **Falling Leaves**

Page 102 • **Mouse House Route**

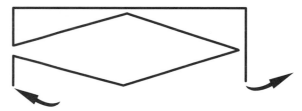

Page 103 ● **Escape from Mr. Mole**

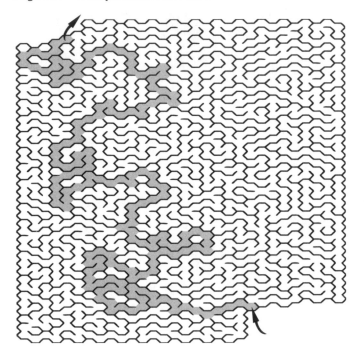

Page 104 ● **Carrots and Apples**

	Carrots	Apples
Lake	2	0
Tree House	2	3
Farm	3	5
Castle	1	3

Page 106 • **Thumbelina's Crossword**

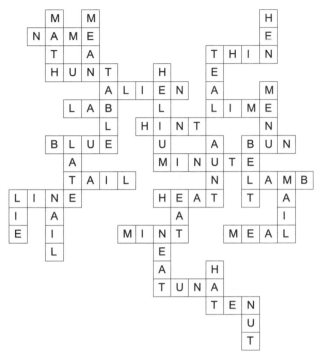

Page 108 • **Wedding Invitation Lists**

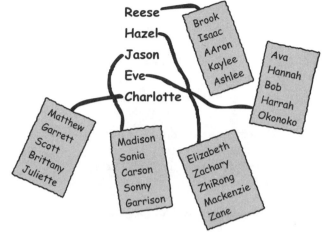

Matthew, Garrett, Scott, Brittany, Juliette, Charlotte: all have TT.

Madison, Sonia, Carson, Sonny, Garrison, Jason: all have SON.

Elizabeth, Zachary, ZhiRong, Mackenzie, Zane, Hazel: all have a Z.

Ava, Hannah, Bob, Harrah, Okonoko, Eve: all are palindromes—they read the same backward or forward.

Brook, Isaac, Aaron, Kaylee, Ashlee, Reese: all have a repeated vowel.

Other Everything® Kids' Titles Available

The Everything® Kids' Animal Puzzle & Activity Book
1-59337-305-8

The Everything® Kids' Baseball Book, 4th Ed.
1-59337-614-6

The Everything® Kids' Bible Trivia Book
1-59337-031-8

The Everything® Kids' Bugs Book
1-58062-892-3

The Everything® Kids' Cars and Trucks
Puzzle & Activity Book
1-59337-703-7

The Everything® Kids' Christmas Puzzle
& Activity Book
1-58062-965-2

The Everything® Kids' Cookbook
1-58062-658-0

The Everything® Kids' Crazy Puzzles Book
1-59337-361-9

The Everything® Kids' Dinosaurs Book
1-59337-360-0

The Everything® Kids' First Spanish Puzzle & Activity Book
1-59337-717-7

The Everything® Kids' Halloween Puzzle &
Activity Book
1-58062-959-8

The Everything® Kids' Hidden Pictures Book
1-59337-128-4

The Everything® Kids' Horses Book
1-59337-608-1

The Everything® Kids' Joke Book
1-58062-686-6

The Everything® Kids' Knock Knock Book
1-59337-127-6

The Everything® Kids' Learning Spanish Book
1-59337-716-9

The Everything® Kids' Math Puzzles Book
1-58062-773-0

The Everything® Kids' Mazes Book
1-58062-558-4

The Everything® Kids' Money Book
1-58062-685-8

The Everything® Kids' Nature Book
1-58062-684-X

The Everything® Kids' Pirates Puzzle and Activity Book
1-59337-607-3

The Everything® Kids' Presidents Book
1-59869-262-3

The Everything® Kids' Princess Puzzle & Activity Book
1-59337-704-5

The Everything® Kids' Puzzle Book
1-58062-687-4

The Everything® Kids' Riddles & Brain Teasers Book
1-59337-036-9

The Everything® Kids' Science Experiments Book
1-58062-557-6

The Everything® Kids' Sharks Book
1-59337-304-X

The Everything® Kids' Soccer Book
1-58062-642-4

The Everything® Kids' States Book
1-59869-263-1

The Everything® Kids' Travel Activity Book
1-58062-641-6